RENEWING LOCAL DEMOCRACY?

BOOKS OF RELATED INTEREST

MANAGING LOCAL SERVICES
From CCT to Best Value
Edited by George A. Boyne

LOCAL GOVERNMENT REORGANISATION
The Review and its Aftermath
Edited by Steve Leach

QUANGOS AND LOCAL GOVERNMENT
A Changing World
Edited by Howard Davis

FINANCING EUROPEAN LOCAL GOVERNMENTS
Edited by John Gibson and Richard Batley

THE POLITICAL EXECUTIVE
Politicians and Management in European Local Government
Edited by Richard Batley and Adrian Campbell

UNDERSTANDING THE SWEDISH MODEL
Edited by Jan-Erik Lane

Renewing Local Democracy?

The Modernisation Agenda in British Local Government

Editor

LAWRENCE PRATCHETT

De Montfort University

FRANK CASS

LONDON • PORTLAND, OR

First published in 2000 in Great Britain by
FRANK CASS AND COMPANY LIMITED
Newbury House, 900 Eastern Avenue, London IG2 7HH, England

and in the United States of America by
FRANK CASS PUBLISHERS
5804 N.E. Hassalo Street,
Portland, Oregon 97213-3644

Website: www.frankcass.co

British Library Cataloguing in Publication Data

Renewing local democracy? The modernisation agenda in
British local government
1.Local government – Great Britain 2.Local government –
Great Britain – Administration
I.Pratchett, Lawrence
320.8'0941

ISBN 0 7146 5046 3 (hb)
ISBN 0 7146 8095 8 (pb)

Library of Congress Cataloging-in-Publication Data

Renewing local democracy? the modernisation agenda in British local
government / editor, Lawrence Pratchett.
    p.   cm.
ISBN 0-7146-5046-3. – ISBN 0-7146-8095-8 (paper)
1.Local government – Great Britain. I. Pratchett, Lawrence.
JS3111.R44   1999
352. 14'0941–dc21   99-40343
                                                                CIP

This group of studies first appeared in a Special Issue on
'Renewing Local Democracy? The Modernisation Agenda in British Local
Government' of *Local Goverment Studies*, Vol.25, No.4 (Winter 1999),
(ISSN 0300-3930) published by Frank Cass..

Printed in Great Britain by Antony Rowe Ltd., Chippenham, Wiltshire

Contents

Introduction: Defining Democratic Renewal

LAWRENCE PRATCHETT

'Democratic renewal' is an ingenious title for the current programme of modernisation in local government. As a phrase it captures both the perceived problems with the existing institutions of local government and the ambitions of the current reform process. It suggests that local democracy is failing and that new proposals will address these failings in order to revitalise democratic practice. In this context 'democratic renewal' has a precise meaning: it is about adjusting the institutions of local government to make them more democratic. At a broader level, however, the phrase also has a much wider attraction. On the one hand it is ideologically neutral, making it difficult for any political party to oppose the overall ambition of reform even if they take issue with some of its detail. Like 'motherhood and apple-pie' democracy has widespread normative appeal and it follows that renewal of democracy has equally widespread support. On the other hand, the concept of democracy, and equally its renewal, is inherently ambiguous. Political theorists have long since struggled to define democracy in any way other than as a broad set of principles (Held, 1996; Beetham, 1996). Translating these principles into practice is continuously beset by problems (Stoker, 1996). As both a descriptive phrase and as an organising concept for the modernisation of local government, therefore, 'democratic renewal' has the advantage of meaning all things to all people. The spirit captured by the phrase has universal appeal although its interpretation may vary greatly in different contexts.

This volume is concerned with both the general spirit of democratic renewal and the detailed proposals for modernising local government which constitute the agenda for reform. It brings together a collection of articles around the common theme of democratic renewal.[1] Some authors concentrate upon specific aspects of the modernisation programme and examine the assumptions that underpin particular proposals and the opportunities and tensions that arise from them. Others take a more overarching view of the renewal process and are thus able to analyse the coherence of the plans and their relationships to broader constitutional change. Each contributor brings a different perspective to the debate, some

Lawrence Pratchett, De Montfort University

of which are complementary to one another, but many of which are contradictory. It is interesting, however, that no contributor argues against the need for democratic renewal, or against the overall spirit which the phrase captures. Differences occur at the level of interpretation and implementation rather than in the overarching ambition. Indeed, while the critique of democratic renewal which this collection of articles develops is derived from many different perspectives, there is one over-riding theme which pervades all the contributions: that the government's proposals do not match their ambitions. All contributors to this volume share a common belief in the need for democratic renewal but question, in different ways, the ability of the current plans to deliver such renewal. Such criticisms are not necessarily negative and many of the contributors applaud the overall ambition of modernisation. In developing a critique of the current proposals and the factors which may inhibit their success, however, these contributors seek to engage specifically with aspects of the renewal programme as part of a broader debate about the role and value of local democracy. This collection, therefore, analyses the specific proposals for modernisation within a broad consensus of the wisdom for democratic renewal.

This introductory article has two main sections. First, it sets the context for the articles which follow by offering various definitions of democratic renewal. Second, it introduces the other contributions to this volume and explains the logic behind the order in which they are presented.

THREE DEFINITIONS OF DEMOCRATIC RENEWAL

The term 'democratic renewal' can be used in at least three ways. First, it can be defined as a set of practical responses to clearly identifiable problems with local democracy. Such a definition focuses attention upon discrete problems (for example, low electoral turnout) and encourages new processes aimed at addressing these individual failings in local democracy (for example, the reform of electoral registration processes). Second, it can be used to discuss more systemic failings in the practice of local democracy and subsequent attempts to instigate broader political, cultural and constitutional change across society. This wider definition focuses attention upon current understandings of the role and purpose of local government and the nature of local democracy as a core component of modern government. Finally, it can be used in a normative sense to describe a new mode of democracy in which different components of representative, deliberative and direct democracy are combined to create a more open, participative and responsive polity at the local level. These definitions are not mutually exclusive of one another and, indeed, have in common the assumption that renewal is both necessary and desirable. They also share similar prescriptions about the way in which existing problems can be remedied. Where they differ is in the scope of reform that they propose and in the wider implications that they hold for democratic practice. This section explores each of these definitions in turn.

Practical Solutions for Perceived Problems

The crisis of local democracy in the UK is well documented (see Cochrane, 1993; King and Stoker, 1996; Pratchett and Wilson, 1996 for recent accounts) and does not require detailed exploration here. For the purposes of setting the current proposals for democratic renewal in context, however, it is useful to describe briefly the central criticisms of current democratic practice by grouping them into three categories: electoral apathy, functional impotence and arcane decision-making structures.

- *Electoral apathy* concerns the persistently low levels of turnout which afflict local elections and the general culture of indifference to local politics which characterises many areas. Overall turnout in the May 1999 local elections was just 32 per cent: poor even by local government's consistently low levels. It is little consolation for elected local government that the subsequent European elections (June 1999) received even less support from citizens (less than 25 per cent). Voter apathy and a general culture of indifference to local politics calls into question both the extent to which councils can claim to represent their communities and their broader legitimacy to govern.

- *Functional impotence* concerns the inability of local authorities to vary their functions or the way in which they are delivered. The application of national standards, benchmarking, the use of arms-length organisations for the delivery of many local services and the increasing prominence of many other agencies in the local arena, all place restrictions upon the ability of individual local authorities to shape their communities. The highly restrictive financial regime which prevents local authorities from exceeding centrally determined standard spending assessments further compounds this problem: if local authorities are unable to vary policies or services according to local demands then it is little wonder that the public are indifferent to local politics and democracy.

- Finally the *arcane decision-making structures*, of which the committee system is the central culprit, further undermines democratic processes. While superficially democratic insofar as all members have equal status in meetings, the committee system has come under increasing attack in recent years for making excessive demands on councillor time while at the same time being an inefficient and ineffective means of managing the business of local government (Audit Commission, 1990, 1997; Game and Leach, 1996). The widespread practice of party groups meeting in private to agree their own positions on each item before the committee meeting only serves further to undermine the democratic credentials of existing political management structures, lending an air of secrecy (if not conspiracy) to the process. The consequence is that local government is seen by many to be bureaucratic, inward looking and unresponsive to the needs of citizens.

These three broad criticisms of electoral apathy, functional impotence and arcane decision-making structures are by no means comprehensive and, indeed, are not universally accepted. John Stewart, for example, has consistently argued that local government has achieved a high level of diversity in services despite increasing centralisation (Stewart, 1989, 1995 *inter alia*). Likewise, there are many examples of local authorities doing things differently from this crude characterisation, with more than two-thirds of local authorities rationalising their committee structures to make them more efficient (LGMB, 1996), and many others developing new political management structures to make decision-making more effective (LGA, 1999). Collectively, therefore, such criticisms are a gross exaggeration of the problems that beset local government, and largely ignore their many achievements of recent years. Nevertheless, they do amount to a conventional wisdom that there is a growing democratic deficit in local government: one which is in urgent need of resolution. In short, there is a concern that specific institutions of local democracy are failing and a broader unease about the nature of local democracy and the ability of local government to deliver it.

It is in this context that the government's proposals for addressing specific problems with local democracy amount to a process of democratic renewal. The 1998 White Paper *Modern Local Government: In Touch with the People* (DETR, 1998) spells out a number of initiatives, each of which address specific failings in existing democratic practice. These can be grouped into four main initiatives:

1. *Electoral reform.* This involves improving the electoral process to enhance opportunities for participation in voting and raising electoral turnout. It includes proposals to improve voter registration procedures, introduce different voting opportunities (for example, on different days or in different locations), experiment with electronic voting systems and possibly to reform the overall electoral process by introducing some form of proportional representation. Collectively this set of proposals addresses the problem of low electoral turnout and voter apathy.

2. *Enhancing public participation.* This involves a set of proposals to enhance public participation in local government by encouraging local authorities to develop a range of consultation and participation techniques, often linked to service improvements in Best Value. Many authorities are already actively pursuing this agenda (see Leach and Wingfield in this volume). While different techniques provide different opportunities for involvement, this aspect of the renewal agenda seeks to address further the democratic deficit associated with citizen apathy and indifference by encouraging local authorities to take the initiative in democratic renewal.

3. *Improving political management.* Proposals to introduce a Westminster style of government into councils by creating a clear separation of executive from assembly are more developed than any other aspect of the democratic renewal agenda. Spelt out in more detail in the 1999 consultation paper *Local Leadership: Local Choice* and the draft *Local Government (Organisation and Standards) Bill* (DETR, 1999), these proposals include opportunities for directly elected mayors in some areas. They have attracted considerable criticism as being an urban agenda which will be largely unworkable in many smaller rural authorities. Nevertheless, it is apparent that their overall aim is to address the excesses of the committee system by introducing clearer, more transparent and accountable leadership in local government.

4. *Extending local autonomy and community leadership.* Finally, there are proposals to charge local authorities with a general duty to promote the economic, social and environmental well-being of their areas. Such a duty strikes right to the heart of the functional impotence of local government by giving authorities the opportunity to pursue any policy, perhaps in collaboration or partnership with other agencies, provided that they can demonstrate how such policies contribute to the economic, social or environmental well-being of their areas. These proposals are the least well developed of the various components that comprise democratic renewal.

As a package of modernisation measures, these four sets of proposals each address specific deficiencies in existing democratic practice. In isolation, however, no one set of measures will greatly extend local democracy – for example, it is evident that simply increasing electoral turnout does not make local government intrinsically more democratic. Indeed, no individual measure is a panacea for the broad range of problems which are seen to be afflicting local democracy. It is the comprehensive nature of these proposals – the attempt to address a range of problems simultaneously – which promises to deliver democratic renewal. In this respect it is important to look beyond the specific proposals, and their respective advantages and disadvantages, and examine the overall spirit of democratic renewal which underpins the detail of modernisation. This leads to the second interpretation of democratic renewal as more systemic failings in the practice of local democracy and attempts to instigate broader political, cultural and constitutional change in response to them.

Broad Political, Cultural and Constitutional Change

This interpretation requires local democracy to be seen within the context of a broader polity: problems at the local level do not simply indicate failure in the institutions of local government but are symptomatic of wider failings in democratic culture and practice. Thus, local government is not so much the weak link in an otherwise effective democracy but rather a model of the broader problems afflicting government at all levels. Moreover, in being singled out for comprehensive renewal, local democracy can be seen as having a central role to play in addressing these broader problems of democracy. From this perspective, therefore, democratic renewal is not really about the largely mechanistic solutions contained in the government's recent pronouncements. These are simply a means to an end. It is more about renewing democratic understanding within communities, encouraging political awareness and enhancing opportunities for political participation.

This second definition of democratic renewal does not discard the current initiatives: indeed, they are central to it. However, the fundamental problem being addressed is notably different. Whereas the first interpretation pointed to specific failings in democratic practices, this second interpretation points to a systemic failing in the attitudes, beliefs and behaviour of citizens in relation to democracy. The problem being addressed, therefore, is not a failing in the formal institutions of democracy but a more deep-rooted failing in the relationship of citizens with the institutions of government. Defined in this way the problems are not inherent in one level of government or, indeed, in specific features of government. Rather, the problems are associated with the perception that there is a growing separation of social and political life – a separation which has led to a disinterest in traditional modes of political participation, a mistrust of elected representatives (and the public sector more generally), and an indifference towards the rights and responsibilities of citizens in a democracy.

The normative basis of this last point needs further examination. As has already been observed, declining numbers of citizens choose to exercise their *rights* to democratic participation. The decreasing turnouts in local, national and European elections are simply the most obvious sign of a more deep-rooted disengagement from political life in many communities. Even fewer see democratic participation as a *responsibility* to be exercised seriously and earnestly, not simply as an expression of personal preferences and opinions but also as a responsible contribution to the welfare and governance of the community. The problem, therefore, is one in which communities and, more importantly, individuals within these communities, no longer understand or contribute to the operation of complex structures of governance. The institutions of government and the democratic processes that are fundamental to these institutions are out of step with the expectations and practices of the communities which they serve. In other words, political processes have become alienated from the day to day activities of community life. Political disengagement is the manifestation of this systemic failing in contemporary democracy.

In this context democratic renewal is about rekindling democratic understanding and awareness within communities. This requires more than simply encouraging higher turnouts in elections or providing alternative opportunities for participation. It is also about going beyond such largely passive measures in order to stimulate political activity by emphasising not only the rights of every citizen within the democratic process but also their responsibilities. Consequently, this second interpretation places a proactive role on local government, imploring them to promote democracy zealously not only through enhancing opportunity but also by providing the catalyst for greater democratic activity. Writing in the middle of the last century, such a proactive role was central to J.S. Mill's understanding of the role of government (Mill, 1998: 229):

> We have now, therefore, obtained a foundation for a twofold division of the merit which any set of political institutions can possess. It consists partly of the degree in which they promote the general mental advancement of the community, including under that phrase advancement in intellect, in virtue, and in practical activity and efficiency; and partly of the degree of perfection with which they organize the moral, intellectual, and active worth already existing, so as to operate with the greatest effect on public affairs.

Mill's view of local government as the ideal location for political education is, of course, well documented (cf. Sharpe, 1970; Hill, 1974). However, given that he was writing under very different political circumstances and addressing very different problems (for example, how to introduce Western democracy into 'savage races') it is surprising, if not indeed alarming, to discover how apposite his remarks are to the current state of democratic government in the UK. Democratic renewal is very much about using the existing institutions of government, and especially local government, to promote the general mental advancement of the community: perhaps not in its pure utilitarian sense but certainly as regards the virtues of democratic practice. Indeed, as Hilary Armstrong emphasises in her article, a central assumption of the current modernisation agenda is that greater public involvement in local affairs will make local governance more effective. Democratic renewal, therefore, is about using local government both to educate communities in politics by giving them greater experience of political life and to stimulate democratic activity across the community. This also fits with the burgeoning literature on social capital which stresses the need for institutionalisation of community relations as a cornerstone of effective social and economic life (Hall, 1999; Putnam, 1993), as well as for more effective governance (Boix and Posner, 1998; see also Lowndes in this volume).

This conclusion becomes particularly apparent when some of the broader constitutional changes being proposed are taken into account. Alongside the specific proposals discussed above for engendering greater democratic participation are also a range of measures aimed at both enhancing citizen education and broadening political interest and activity. Moves to enhance citizen education are most obvious in the proposals to include citizenship as a core component of the national curriculum. Beyond this there are also attempts to improve the standing of the public sector. New awards for successful teachers and the creation of 'super nurses' in the health service are symptomatic of the broader aim of making public service more appealing. Similarly, the attempt to create a new ethical framework for local government reflects the government's concern to emphasise the highest standards in public life. Moves to broaden political interest and activity include such diverse initiatives as the government's commitment to a Freedom of Information Act and even more fundamental attempts to alter the UK constitution. The creation of the Scottish parliament and the Welsh assembly, and proposals to reform the House of Lords, are the most obvious examples here. The government's keen interest in electoral reform also serves as an example in this area, although the extent to which this interest is prompted by political expedience rather than ideological commitment to democratic renewal is questionable. That many of these initiatives have been diluted or dissipated by vested interests and political prudence should not detract from the overall ambition of modernisation. The ambition of reform should not be confused with the process. The potential for a wide range of measures to contribute to democratic renewal is evident. In this respect modernisation is as much about changing the expectations and behaviour of citizens within the existing institutions of democracy as it is about changing the structures and functions of government. The success or failure of democratic renewal needs to be assessed against the overall achievements of a broad range of initiatives rather than against the success or failure of specific events.

A New Mode of Local Democracy

The final interpretation of democratic renewal follows closely from an understanding of the process as being concerned with changing the attitudes and behaviour of citizens, because it concentrates upon the new mix of institutions and practices which the modernisation process introduces. The first definition of democratic renewal concentrated upon a discrete set of proposals, each of which addresses specific failings in contemporary democracy. The second emphasises that it is also about a broader strategy which seeks to draw upon existing institutions in order to alter citizen attitudes and their relations with structures of governance. This third interpretation is even more radical, suggesting a new democratic polity which not only improves the effectiveness of existing practices but also draws upon different components of direct, consultative, deliberative and representative democracy to create a new democratic order. The point is not that some of these components contribute more to democracy than others. Rather, it is the successful combination of them that makes for the new mode of democracy which the renewal process offers. Combining different components in this way is inevitably problematic and there is a range of tensions that emerge. It is useful first, however, to examine the different components of the mix before analysing the problems which may emerge from combining them.

There can be little doubt that the democratic renewal agenda encourages aspects of direct democracy. The most obvious example of this is in the increased use of referendums as the basis of local decision-making on some important issues, although developments in user management of services are also significant here. The key feature of direct democracy in this context is that it passes power and responsibility for specific decisions to the community. The best example of this has been in relation to the constitutional changes in Scotland, Wales and Northern Ireland, all of which have been premised on a referendum to endorse change. Likewise, the decision to introduce a mayor and assembly for London involved a referendum in which the majority of those voting supported the principle of a Greater London Authority. The use of referendums for other decisions is also growing. It seems likely that many communities will be given the opportunity to vote in a referendum on whether their local authority should have a directly elected mayor (DETR, 1999). Indeed, Watford has already committed to such an action once the relevant legislation is in place (probably 2000). Similarly, several local authorities have used referendums for reaching key decisions: in Neath for considering the future of the town council; in Buxworth (Derbyshire) for considering a name change; and in Milton Keynes for setting the 1999 budget. All of these have been hailed as major achievements in extending democracy, allowing citizens to participate directly in fundamental decisions which affect them. The Milton Keynes referendum, which asked voters to choose between three council tax increases (5 per cent, 9.8 per cent or 15 per cent), boasted a turnout of 44.7 per cent (out of a 149,241 voters) compared with one of just 26.2 per cent in the previous local elections. The Buxworth referendum, which asked 600 residents to vote on a change of name for their village (a surprisingly contentious issue), achieved a turnout of almost two-thirds (62 per cent) of eligible voters.

Such direct democracy, however, is not without its problems. The Milton Keynes referendum did not gain a simple majority for any one of its options although the council's preferred option (not surprisingly, the middle of the three options) received the single largest proportion (46 per cent) of the vote. In other words, only 21 per cent of Milton Keynes residents voted in favour of the final budget package, while almost 24 per cent actually voted against it. In London, despite an overwhelming 'yes' vote (72 per cent) the turnout was only 31.5 per cent – as a consequence, less than a quarter of eligible people (22 per cent) actually voted in favour of the Greater London Authority, although even fewer voted against it (8.7 per cent). If referendums suffer from the same low turnouts as elections, or fail to achieve a simple majority for a particular decision, then their effectiveness as a tool for community expression is blunted. In such instances this form of democracy, far from being even tyranny of the majority, becomes the tyranny of a minority over the majority. The other problem with referendums is that the options inevitably must be limited to a few clearly distinguishable choices. Despite claims that the Milton Keynes referendum raised the profile of the council's budget setting process the choices were limited to three discrete increases, each of which had hypothecated service cuts or improvements linked to them. Such problems are compounded by allegations that those asking the questions will inevitably shape the answers. Opposition members levelled this criticism at the Milton Keynes referendum. The government is also clearly concerned that those authorities forced by legislation to hold a referendum on new political management structures will deliberately bias the question – hence the caveat that all referendum questions will have to be approved by the Secretary of State (DETR, 1999: 2.13). The advent of new technologies is widely held to increase the opportunities for direct democracy (Budge, 1996). Of course, it also increases the problems associated with such initiatives (Bellamy and Taylor, 1998).

Within democratic renewal, however, the point of referendums and other forms of direct democracy is that they are only one part of the democratic process. Linked into such initiatives are also attempts to increase opportunities for political participation in other arenas. The new democratic mix also emphasises consultative and deliberative participation as key contributions to modern democracy. Consultative participation is given considerable emphasis in the Best Value framework. While not prescribing the form of participation required of local authorities, the government is clear that service development should be based upon extensive consultation with service users. Indeed, it is apparent that one aim of the democratic renewal process is to make stronger links between the democratic and service delivery functions of public organisations. As the Minister for Local Government states in her article, 'Best Value ties public service more closely to the people'. In this respect, Best Value is about breaking down the barriers between public management and democratic participation. Consulting service users and those otherwise affected by local authority functions is to be an essential component of the new democratic polity. An awareness of this is one reason why so many authorities are experimenting with different forms of consultative participation (Lowndes *et al.*, 1998). Consulting service users, of course, has always been a feature of the new public management. Many of the consumer-oriented mechanisms that emerged in the 1980s were a direct consequence of the application of the new public management in local government (see Leach and Wingfield in this volume). The new focus on consultation does not mean losing the best features of the new public management. It does, however, redress the balance by once again emphasising the need for broader public involvement in setting and evaluating service priorities, standards and processes.

Deliberative participation has less of a history in local government than consultative mechanisms. As Elster (1998: 1) observes, deliberative democracy concerns more than simply 'decision making by discussion among free and equal citizens'. It also involves 'the idea that democracy revolves around the *transformation* rather than simply the *aggregation* of preferences' (emphasis added). Consequently, while concepts of deliberative democracy have been widely discussed within political science (cf. Barber, 1984; Dryzek, 1990; Habermas, 1996) their application in UK local government has been treated with some suspicion. Case studies of deliberative exercises have emphasised the difficulties of ensuring adequate representation of views across the community, the dangers of issues being captured by particularly vocal and articulate groups, and the problems that arise from attempting to include sections of the community which are not accustomed to participation in such events. Nevertheless, interest in deliberative democracy has grown considerably in recent years (Lowndes *et al.*, 1998). From the now ubiquitous 'focus groups' to more ambitious attempts at 'visioning', and even experimentation with 'citizens' juries', a majority of local authorities have included some form of deliberative participation in their public participation strategies. Despite the recognised expense associated with deliberative exercises, however, few contribute to clear-cut outcomes. Rather, the experience of many is that participants learn more about the complexities of local government and the views of their fellow participants. In this respect the value of deliberation is in the actual participation. Activities such as 'visioning' can be very effective in building consensus across communities (Pratchett, 1999). They can also serve as a means of 'educating' citizens in civic values by providing valuable experience of political participation. Consequently, deliberative participation as currently practised in local government serves two potential functions: the 'education' of citizens and the 'transformation' of views through discussion.

In so far as deliberative exercises achieve these two aims they have much to commend them. As a means of enhancing the decision-making capacities of local government, however, they are more limited. Again, however, the point is that deliberative participation is not supposed to be the sole means of extending democracy. Rather, it is another component to set alongside aspects of direct and representative democracy. To complement this process, therefore, renewal of the institutions of representative democracy is also necessary. The specific reforms mentioned earlier and, especially, the new political management arrangements being imposed on local government are parts of this renewal process. Of particular importance in this context, however, is the government's emphasis not only upon creating clearer and stronger executive leadership in local government but also its corresponding emphasis on 'powerful roles for all councillors' (DETR, 1999). Under the new political management arrangements elected members will be expected to concentrate even more upon their roles as representatives of the community. The proposals suggest not only a role for members as advocates of community preferences but also as a catalyst for community action. Councillors will be expected not only to articulate the needs of their wards but also to participate more effectively in them. Representative democracy in this form is not premised solely upon the ballot box, it also involves ensuring a continuous dialogue between elected members and the communities that they represent.

Bringing the different strands of the new democratic order together is not an easy task. It is more than simply ensuring that there are components of direct, consultative, deliberative and representative forms present in the new polity. It is more, even, than ensuring that there is an adequate balance between the different components and the way in which they affect democratic processes – although achieving such a balance is, in itself, fraught with difficulties. More than this, it is also about managing the tensions which combining such different components inevitably gives rise to. One set of tensions revolves around how different components should be mixed to resolve particular issues. Where different components emphasise different outcomes which aspect should take precedence? For example, should a referendum which is inevitably limited to a few discrete choices be binding upon elected representatives who may have access to more timely and relevant information than those voting? On the other hand, should elected representatives have the right to over-rule the wishes of the majority of voters as demonstrated in a referendum? Such complexities are compounded further when the outcomes of deliberative exercises are added to the equation, possibly expressing other preferences and suggesting other options.

Another set of tensions revolves around reconciling conflicts of interest within communities. There is an implicit assumption within many discussions of deliberative democracy that communities are homogeneous entities which can achieve consensus through discussion of their preferences (see, for example, New Economics Foundation, 1999). Case study evidence also suggests, however, that encouraging enhanced public participation can also emphasise differences within communities, lead to greater parochialism and exacerbate cleavages across communities (Lowndes et al., 1998). There is also the danger that the renewal process will raise unrealistic expectations of what can be achieved within communities, leading to even greater disillusionment with democracy in general and local politics in particular. While such problems are far from being a certainty – and, indeed, can be overcome with careful management – the potential exists for democratic renewal to backfire on itself. Failure to develop the appropriate mix of direct, consultative, deliberative and representative mechanisms will leave the renewal process impoverished and incomplete. However, failure to manage the inevitable tensions of mixing these various components could be far more disastrous in that it could lead to a complete alienation of citizens from the institutions of local democracy.

THE STRUCTURE OF THIS VOLUME

The purpose of this collection is three-fold. First, it aims to contribute to the debate around democratic renewal by clarifying its meaning and relevance as a current policy. Second, it seeks to develop a critique of the current renewal project by focusing on both the detail of the agenda and its broader implications. Third, it aims to bring together recent empirical evidence that supports or enhances understanding of the democratic renewal project and its implicit tensions. All of the articles which follow contribute to one or more of these aims. Having introduced the different ways in which democratic renewal can be interpreted and alerted the reader to the recurrent themes which cut across the critiques developed here, this final section introduces the articles themselves and the logic of their order.

Following this introductory piece the first article is by the Minister for Local Government, Hilary Armstrong MP, and sets out the government's main thinking behind the White Paper *Modern Local Government: In Touch with the People* (DETR, 1998). The text is an edited version of a speech given to the seminar on which this volume is based, which took place soon after the publication of the government's White Paper. It is necessary to read the article in this context. The government's thinking on many of these issues has been refined since this text was prepared and has been supplemented by several other consultation papers and draft bills. Nevertheless, the article is useful because it provides a snapshot of the government's thinking at the time. If the White Paper is seen as the foundations of the democratic renewal project then this article must be seen as the architect's explanation of why the foundations are laid out in the way they are. At the very minimum Hilary Armstrong's summary of the government's position on democratic renewal provides a historical record which is useful as a basis for understanding the development and implementation of the policy as it stood in September 1998. More than this, however, the article also sets out four key themes which endure beyond the precise detail of the modernisation proposals. At a later date these themes may well form an appropriate basis for evaluating the success or failure of the government in this important policy area.

The remaining articles concentrate upon different aspects of the democratic renewal agenda. Gray and Jenkins adopt a historical approach to the subject to investigate the extent to which the renewal agenda represents continuity in the institutions of local government rather than change. They argue that a central problem for democratic renewal is the sense of alienation experienced by most citizens in relation to local government. Alienation not simply in terms of remoteness but also in terms of the extent to which citizens feel powerless and disengaged from local government: citizens doubt the ability of conventional democratic means to have any effect. Democratic renewal, they argue, needs to address this alienation by showing that participation in local government can have some positive effects. The problem, however, is that the absence of local autonomy contributes to the sense of meaninglessness in local politics. At the heart of their argument, therefore, is the assertion that the government has failed to define the problem properly and that, consequently, their solution will evolve as a 'fudged orthodoxy'.

The following two papers concentrate particularly upon the public participation aspects of the renewal agenda. Leach and Wingfield's contribution summarises recent research into public participation initiatives in local government and notes the wide range of experience which already exists. As their title suggests, however, there are real concerns over the extent to which this aspect of modernisation will become marginalised in the race to implement other more tangible elements of the agenda. At the heart of their argument is the concern that there are a number of implicit tensions which militate against local authorities continuing to experiment with public participation when other aspects of the agenda are being given much greater prominence.

The contribution from Barnes follows neatly from Leach and Wingfield in so far as it develops a framework for understanding the full value of public participation in democratic organisations. Barnes' project is to move the evaluation of participation beyond positivist models of success or failure to concentrate upon the broader benefits of participation. To this end she offers a range of dimensions along which participation may vary and develops a framework which concentrates as much upon process as it does upon outcomes. Her contribution complements that of Leach and Wingfield because it clearly demonstrates the broader benefits to be gained from enhanced public participation. Consequently, it is, in effect, an argument in favour of prioritising the participatory features of democratic renewal.

The following two articles move to another aspect of the renewal agenda: that of political leadership. Copus concentrates upon the role of the party group in conventional local government and argues that the government's failure to address such activities explicitly is an oversight which may eventually undermine the democratic renewal project. He emphasises a distinction between the presence of party politics and the existence of party groups in local government. While there are considerable benefits in the former, it is the latter with which he takes issue. Party groups, he argues, enforce party political loyalty above all other considerations. While this may have been an effective means of organising party politics under the committee system, rigid adherence to party group politics will serve to undermine the effective separation of executive from assembly. His concern is that a failure to reorganise party groups to take account of the new roles could lead to a situation in which 'only symbolic scrutiny (of the executive) would occur by majority party back-benchers who had previously discussed and decided upon issues in group'. In this worst case scenario power would become even more centralised with even fewer opportunities for community input to the governance of localities.

The John and Cole article complements the contribution of Copus by offering comparative cases studies of six council leaders in England and

France. Like Copus, they observe the limitations which party groups
currently impose upon leaders in British local government. Their concern,
however, is not so much with how leadership might be distorted by party
groups but more with the factors which enable leaders to be successful.
They build a typology of leadership around two dimensions: a distinction
between 'responsive' and 'directive leaders'; and a distinction between
'power to' and 'power over'. They conclude that French city leaders find it
much easier to act as visionaries for their areas because party constraints are
weaker. At the same time, however, they also emphasise the importance of
the character and abilities of individuals in effecting their own leadership
success. The lessons that they implicitly draw for democratic renewal,
therefore, are twofold. First, for successful executive leadership to emerge
the excesses of party control will need to be broken down in British local
government. Second, even if such barriers are removed, the emergence of
effective leaders is not guaranteed. The emergence of individuals with the
right qualities (however that is defined) is as much a matter of fate as it is
of institutional design or political culture.

The final article by Lowndes brings attention back to the broad ambition
of democratic renewal and the way in which it is implemented. She sees the
concept of trust as being central to New Labour's policy approach. Her
article uses this concept to explore the changing nature of central–local
government relations during the evolution of the modernisation project. She
draws upon a range of sources to show how there is a fundamental
incompatibility between the government's own conception of trust and that
held by local government. The former sees trust as a prize to be earned from
modernisation, while the latter perceives it to be a fundamental starting
point for democratic renewal. This incompatibility lies at the heart of the
current frustration being displayed by both sides as the democratic renewal
project unfolds. Ultimately, however, she implies that a new relationship of
trust will emerge only when both sides concede some ground. 'Trust cannot
be built solely on the basis of a bargain or a principle – in fact, it grows out
of ongoing interaction and learning.' Central government needs to
demonstrate its acceptance of the principle that local government is to be
trusted at the same time as local government proves it can be trusted. It is a
'chicken and egg' dilemma which lies at the heart of local government
modernisation.

Democratic renewal, as defined here, has the potential to be one of the
most radical policies of New Labour's first term in office. At its best it
promises to change fundamentally the relationship between citizens, their
communities and broader structures of government. It suggests a renewal of
democracy not only within local government but also across a whole range
of institutions by ushering in a new democratic polity which effectively

combines elements of direct, deliberative and representative democracy. At the same time, however, such an ambitious project is also plagued by contradictions, tensions and ambiguities. Collectively, the articles presented in this volume provide a broad critique of the democratic renewal project. Their purpose is not to provide a comprehensive review of the process and its success or failure – that will have to wait for a later date. Rather, they provide a collection of insights into aspects of the agenda, thereby illuminating both the process and its tensions. In so doing they make an important contribution to the debate around a key programme of reform – one which, if successful, has profound implications not only for local government but also for the broader practice of democracy in the UK.

NOTES

1. Earlier versions of the majority of these articles were first presented at a seminar on democratic renewal organised jointly by the Urban Politics and Public Administration specialist groups of the Political Studies Association (CIPFA offices, London, 23 September 1998). I am grateful to Janice Macmillan and Andrew Massey for their assistance in co-ordinating that event and to all participants for their contributions to the discussions which led to the refinement of the articles presented here.

REFERENCES

Audit Commission, 1990, *We Can't go on Meeting Like This* (London: HMSO).
Audit Commission, 1997, *Representing the People* (London: HMSO).
Barber, B., 1984, *Strong Democracy: Participatory Politics for a New Age* (London: University of California Press).
Beetham, D., 1996, 'Theorising Democracy and Local Government', in King and Stoker, 1996.
Bellamy, C. and J. Taylor, 1998, *Governing in the Information Age* (Buckingham: Open University Press).
Boix, C. and D.N. Posner, 1998, 'Social Capital: Explaining its Origins and Effects on Government Performance', *British Journal of Political Science*, 28, pp.686–93.
Budge, I., 1996, *The New Challenge of Direct Democracy* (Oxford: Polity Press).
Cochrane, A., 1993, *Whatever Happened to Local Government?* (Buckingham: Open University Press).
DETR, 1998, *Modern Local Government: In Touch with the People* (London: HMSO) (Cm 4014).
DETR, 1999, *Local Leadership: Local Choice* (London: HMSO) (Cm 4298).
Dryzek, J., 1990, *Discursive Democracy* (Cambridge: Cambridge University Press).
Elster, J. (ed.), 1998, *Deliberative Democracy* (Cambridge: Cambridge University Press).
Game, C. and S. Leach, 1996, 'Political Parties and Local Democracy', in Pratchett and Wilson, 1996.
Habermas, J., 1996, *Between Facts and Norms* (Cambridge, MA: MIT Press).
Hall, P.A., 1999, 'Social Capital in Britain', *British Journal of Political Science*, Vol.29, No.3, pp.417–62.
Held, D., 1996, *Models of Democracy* (Cambridge: Polity Press, 2nd edn).
Hill, D., 1974, *Democratic Theory and Local Government* (London: Allen and Unwin).
King, D. and G. Stoker (eds.), 1996, *Rethinking Local Democracy* (Basingstoke: Macmillan).
LGA, 1999, *Making Decisions Locally* (London: Local Government Association).
LGMB, 1996, *Portrait of Change 1995* (Luton: Local Government Management Board).

Lowndes, V. *et al.*, 1998, *Enhancing Public Participation in Local Government: A Research Report* (London: DETR).

Mill, J.S., 1998, *Considerations on Representative Government*, ed. J. Grey (Oxford: Oxford World Classics, Oxford University Press).

New Economics Foundation, 1999, *Participation Works!* (London: New Economics Foundation).

Pratchett, L. and D. Wilson (eds.), 1996, *Local Democracy and Local Government* (Basingstoke: Macmillan).

Pratchett, L., 1999, 'New Fashions in Public Participation: Towards Greater Democracy?' *Parliamentary Affairs*, Vol.52, No.4.

Putnam, R., 1993, *Making Democracy Work: Civic Traditions in Modern Italy* (Princeton, NJ: Princeton University Press).

Sharpe, L.J., 1970, 'Theories and Values of Local Government', *Political Studies*, 18, pp.153–74.

Stewart, J., 1989, 'A Future for Local Authorities as Community Government', in J. Stewart and G. Stoker (eds.), *The Future of Local Government* (Basingstoke: Macmillan).

Stewart, J., 1995, 'A Future for Local Authorities as Community Government', in J. Stewart and G. Stoker (eds.), *Local Government in the 1990s* (Basingstoke: Macmillan).

Stoker, G., 1996, 'Introduction: Normative Theories of Local Government and Democracy', in King and Stoker, 1996.

The Key Themes of Democratic Renewal

HILARY ARMSTRONG MP

The contents of the Local Government White Paper *Modern Local Government: In Touch with the People* have been widely discussed so I do not intend to spell out its contents in detail or to run through its main proposals here. Instead, I want to use this article to sketch out the political themes which I believe *In Touch with the People* represents and the opportunities for local government which they present. Those themes are:

* redefining the relationship of local government with the people;

* earning public expenditure;

* ending ideological battles over public service provision; and

* innovation in governance.

REDEFINING THE RELATIONSHIP OF LOCAL GOVERNMENT WITH THE PEOPLE

In many ways, the White Paper drew a line in the sand following generations of disintegration in the relationship between central and local government. If the party was over by the mid-1970s, then the 1980s and 1990s represented a substantial and often painful hangover. By 1 May 1997 central/local relations had reached an all-time low.

We should never forget just how bad things had become by the end of the Major government: mutual dislike and mistrust; personal enmity and bitterness; backbiting and buck-passing: and that was just amongst cabinet colleagues! Things were even worse for councils. Dominated by their political opponents, we now know the Conservatives even considered the outright abolition of British local government.

Institutional enmity and mistrust was replaced in May 1997: immediately, with a partnership programme designed to rebuild trust and positive engagement; and subsequently, through consultation and the preparation of the White Paper. It is fashionable for some commentators to paint the government as centralising and distrustful of local councils; as though they were somehow permanently 'off message'. This is simply untrue. If the government had wanted to embark on the destruction of local government, we would have had to do nothing at all. Public apathy and indifference would have done more to undermine local councils than anything government could do. By contrast, the White Paper seeks to address apathy and indifference and to help local government to redefine its relationships with the people.

The political and organisational culture of local government grew out of the early nineteenth century. Little wonder then that at the gateway to the twenty-first century the culture and the service and political models which flow from it are ill-equipped for their purpose. The White Paper aims to change the way local people relate to the provision of local services so that they are involved in setting standards, monitoring performance and evaluating service. Our Best Value proposals will help to achieve that.

It is vital that in strengthening the public service relationship between councils and their communities we recognise that the nature of the service sector has altered immensely over recent years. New technology and new ways of working have changed the expectations people have of the capacity of the service sector to meet their own high standards. The implementation of Best Value by local councils has to reflect those great expectations and go further. Innovation and excellence must be the hallmarks of public service. Freedom from the restrictions of Compulsory Competitive Tendering must not become an excuse for a relaxation of service standards, bad or restrictive practices or poor performance. On the contrary, Best Value is in many ways a tougher regime than CCT. For whilst CCT bound local government with red tape, Best Value ties public service more closely to the people. By getting local services right – and right first time – the relationship with residents will be transformed.

Local government, though, is more than just about how services are delivered. It is about the relationship between local people, place and politics. I believe in vibrant, dynamic local politics. Interesting enough to inspire not just the energy to vote but the enthusiasm to get involved. The White Paper seeks to encourage local councils to consider the interaction between people, place and politics. Local people will be more involved in service delivery. They will be empowered through greater use of local referendums. They will have a bigger say over local spending. Councillors will no longer spend their time explaining the council to local people. Their task will be to represent the people to the council – to be champions of their local areas. Councils will be open, accountable, outward looking, and responsive. All councillors will have important roles.

Crucial to the achievement of this is the separation of the executive function. We could have a long and very interesting debate about the role and structure of an executive. Indeed, the government has welcomed advice from all quarters on the detail of the three frameworks we set out in the White Paper. What is clear is that within each framework there is huge scope for diversity, for a council to adopt the detail structures best suited to its own place and politics.

But I am clear that the key to success will be the role of what we might term the 'back-bench councillor'. We need people from all groups in our communities to come forward and offer their services as councillors. We need to break free from the pattern so often found today where many councillors are relatively old, few are women, and even fewer are drawn from the ethnic minorities. The importance of the back-bench councillor has certainly not got the attention it deserves, largely because it is the issue of mayors which has grabbed the headlines. Councillors need to be able to spend time in their communities. They need to be given the facilities, the training and the guidance they need to bring to the council's decision-making processes a full knowledge of what their local communities need and want.

Place will become more important as councils change and move away from uniformity of structure and function. Councils will provide better leadership for their communities and be responsible for the economic, social and environmental well-being of their areas. Local politics will become more important to local people. The existing political and administrative structures in local government serve to exclude people from their local councils. This is true of just about all forms of government, but it is particularly acute in local government where electoral turn-out has become so low and where the local relationship should be so close.

We have to reignite the enthusiasm of local people in local politics by ending the out-dated, arcane committee system. It is easier to trace the medieval origins of the current committee system than to state its relevance for the twenty-first century. With its cumbersome and corrosive impact on the interest and involvement of local people, the council committee system should be consigned to the history books.

The White Paper will help to do that but local councils have to recognise and embrace change for themselves if they are to genuinely redefine their relationship with the people. There is no point in adopting a model for new political structures which is acceptable to the majority group but unacceptable to the majority of the local population: no point because the new structures should be designed to engage the interest of the people, not to further their sense of exclusion from the local political system; no point either, because the White Paper will empower local people through the use of referendums on establishing an elected mayor. If a local council has to have a new form of local political leadership imposed upon it by the people then it will have lost the initiative.

As councils choose their new forms of political management they should not be seeking to graft on the provisions of the White Paper to their current political process but to think anew about the best means for opening up local politics to local people. The White Paper is not some modernising 'loyalty test' which councils have to pass by hiding the current system under a veneer of modernised respectability. It should be the basis for a fundamental rethink of the way councils work and the way they relate to their residents. Merely rebranding the Policy and Resources Committee as a 'Cabinet' may become a fast-track to a directly elected mayor imposed by the people. Whilst there is no doubt that would indeed redefine an individual local council's relationship with its people, I want to see local councils taking the initiative by pushing change themselves rather than being pushed to change by others.

EARNING PUBLIC EXPENDITURE

Changing the relationship between local councils and local people is a vital element in the modernisation of local government. The way councils think about 'tax and spend' policies is just as important. This brings me to my second theme. The government was elected on a pledge not to increase direct taxation. Fiscal prudence is a discipline rather than a dogma. It is, and remains, an important tool for getting government to think more radically about how it earns and spends public money. In the past, government has been able to solve problems by throwing other people's money at them. It has been too easy to put up taxes rather than prioritise spending. Our commitment not to fall into this 'tax and spend' trap remains intact. It was this discipline which produced the Comprehensive Spending Review and the re-ordering of government expenditure priorities.

The notion that higher taxes and ever greater spending is proof of the power and pride of government is as outdated as the local government committee system. Value for money, earning every penny of public expenditure, payment by results and investment for modernisation – these are the real demonstration of radical and effective government. It is for that reason that each central government department is now expected to agree and deliver three-year public service agreements with the Treasury, governing the performance of public expenditure. This is a transformation in the treatment of public expenditure by central government.

The White Paper allows for a similar local transformation in tax and spend policies. Under capping, councils hardly had to exercise any fiscal prudence themselves. Almost every town hall budget was set in Whitehall – all the spending and all the cutbacks could be blamed on government. We have ended crude, universal council tax capping and propose to replace it with a reserve power to protect the taxpayer. Local councils will, therefore, become responsible for their own fiscal prudence. Just as importantly, our move to a system which provides stability in funding over a three-year period will allow for the development of local public service agreements and a similarly disciplined and prudent financial regime.

Local councils will have to justify their expenditure to the public rather than to the government. They will have to demonstrate, through Best Value, that they are getting value for the public's money and by doing so will be able more easily to earn their public expenditure. Similarly, our proposals for local business rates will make it necessary not just to seek to tax local business but to consult with local business on the nature and scope of that spending.

The White Paper is about moving away from the old politics of 'spend and blame' towards a new relationship between tax raiser and taxpayer, built on a greater degree of mutual understanding between what is expected of both. Government will hold a watching brief. By ending capping, promoting greater stability, localising elements of the business rate – and by making councils more responsible for the real costs of excessive council tax rises – we will give greater local discretion in local taxation. This is not an easy option for local councils. They will find, as we have found, that decisions on expenditure priorities are often difficult and challenging but are always preferable to a knee-jerk return to tax and spend.

ENDING IDEOLOGICAL BATTLES OVER PUBLIC SERVICE PROVISION

The quality, quantity and delivery of local services will be vital to the process of earning public expenditure. That very neatly brings me on to my third theme: ending the ideological battles over public service provision. Public service provision has for too long been the battleground for ideological struggles between the old left and the new right. For the old left, public services were sometimes too statist and uniform, delivered through monolithic bureaucracies. Quality of service sometimes played second fiddle to the producer interest. For the new right, free market domination did not just challenge the inadequacies of under-performance in the public sector but challenged the necessity and the very future of public service provision.

Nowhere is there greater scope for a 'Third Way' than in public services. The old ideologies created conflict rather than competition and collaboration between public and private sectors. Our Best Value proposals seek to take the ideology out of public service provision. Instead, we want to see the formation of new and innovative partnerships between the public and private sectors. Where partnerships are not appropriate we expect genuine and fair competition. We are seeking to create an ongoing relationship between councils and enterprise. To that end, we are proposing changes to local business rates, as I have mentioned, and we are seeking to make partnerships easier to create and PFI (private finance initiative) more effective for meeting local public service objectives.

The battles over the means of service provision are a distraction which public services can do without. They have served to make price more important than performance; deliverer more central than delivery. Our White Paper seeks to end these battles and move instead to public/private partnerships. We want to harness what is best from both to provide the best for all.

INNOVATION IN GOVERNANCE

Innovation in service delivery will be crucial to the development of these new partnerships. The final theme I want to address is innovation in governance. In the past, it has suited Whitehall to see local government as uniform. To view local government as just a form of local administration, as though people, place and politics were somehow the same all over the country. We know that is not the case, but it has been administratively convenient to imagine it was true.

But people, place and politics are different across the country. This government recognises, in a way no other government ever has, that Scotland and Wales are different from England and different from one another. London is different, too, as are the English regions. As a reflection of those differences we are creating different forms of governance.

Local councils can be different from one another, too, reflecting the differences of local people, local places and local politics. That is why the White Paper encourages new forms of local political management in councils across the country, reflecting local differences. Councils should be using the opportunity presented in the White Paper to assert their local differences and to be proud of them. Where local councils are pushing the boundaries of performance, demonstrating their excellence and innovation, government should respond with encouragement and support. That is why our Beacon councils proposal is so important.

Through Beacon councils and Beacon services we can stimulate and encourage innovation. We can promote difference in local government; making sure that councils which use their existing powers will enjoy greater freedom to innovate even further. Beacon councils will have efficient, in-touch political systems enabling them to deliver best value services and to respond quickly and effectively to the demands of the local community. Better contacts with the local community will inspire yet more change and innovation.

Beacons are not an expression of elitism. They are a recognition of excellence and this recognition will not merely be by us in government, but underwritten by an independent advisory panel. They are the means by which the pace of modernisation can be set by the fastest, not held back by the slowest. The first to embrace the modernising agenda will be the first to benefit from it.

Government will make the necessary legislative changes and work to motivate and manage modernisation. Councils should start to modernise now in a whole range of areas. They can develop their role as community leaders; reform local democratic arrangements; prepare for best value; review three year spending plans; and make progress on their need for capital investment.

Councils can also make progress on their political management arrangements. The full separation of the executive from backbench role and establishment of effective arrangements for scrutiny of the executive will require primary legislation. But there is much that can be done now and a number of councils are already streamlining their arrangements.

Spreading good practice will be a key part of the early implementation of the White Paper. So it is a significant step forward that the LGA has published guidance on how local authorities can move towards the adoption of modern political management arrangements within the existing legislative framework. The message for local councils is: do not wait for legislation, but lead change yourselves.

CONCLUDING COMMENT

The government's White Paper does present local councils with the opportunity to bring about their own renaissance. To do that they must redefine their relationship with the public; they have to be earning public expenditure and forming new partnerships for service delivery and development. Innovation and excellence should become watchwords for public service and local governance. All over local government there are councillors and officers with the skills and commitment to meet the challenges and the opportunities which the White Paper represents. All over the country there are individuals and enterprises keen to participate in modernising local government. For the first time in a generation, local government has the opportunity to modernise itself, with government as a force for change rather than an instrument of control. The chance to change is here; the time for change is now.

NOTE

This article is an edited version of a speech given to the Urban Politics/Public Administration Specialist Groups of the Political Studies Association on 23 September 1998. Since then the Government's thinking on many of the issues discussed here has been further developed. This article is included here, however, to give a feel for the Government's thinking on democratic renewal as it existed shortly after the publication of its White Paper *Modern Local Government: In Touch with the People.*

Democratic Renewal in Local Government: Continuity and Change

ANDREW GRAY AND BILL JENKINS

It is to be expected that when a government is elected to replace another, especially after 18 years of office, it will propose a programme of change. Yet change may be difficult to effect, especially if a government has failed to grasp the tensions and ambiguities within its rhetoric. Certainly, as we have described elsewhere (Gray and Jenkins, 1998, 1999), the new Labour government of 1997 has announced an ambitious prospectus of constitutional, policy and administrative change enveloped in a language of modernisation and democratisation. Local government, to a considerable extent a bastion of opposition to the previous government, has an important place within this prospectus, reflected in the prompt announcement of the replacement of compulsory competitive tendering by a regime designed to promote *best value* within local authorities and the publication of a range of consultative and white papers outlining a programme for the democratic renewal of local self-government.

What are the aims of democratic renewal? What are its elements? What does it assume about the place of local government in a democratic unitary state? What are the conditions which democratic renewal in local government is designed to remedy? Are they likely to be effective? These questions and others are important not only for the government as it proceeds with its programme but also for those who wish to understand the implications of democratic renewal both for local government itself and the wider system of government. In seeking to inform answers, this paper proposes that (1) a history of the philosophy of local government illuminates a consideration of the government's proposals, (2) a conceptualisation of (non-)participation in terms of alienation reveals an over-simplification in current government thinking of the relation of participation to democratic renewal, and (3) New Labour's agenda, however reformed, overlooks the continuity of tensions revealed by this history of philosophy of local government and a wider perspective on alienation and, as importantly, needs to relate its position to them explicitly. The remainder

Andrew Gray, University of Durham; Bill Jenkins, University of Kent at Canterbury of this article examines each of these points and links them to the emerging debate on democratic renewal.

LOCAL GOVERNANCE AND LOCAL SELF-GOVERNMENT

All but the smallest nation states have some form of local administration of government. This brings administrative benefits: enhancing operating ability, minimising the financial and physical costs of operating at a distance, and drawing on local knowledge and implementation. It also provides for a binding network of local administration in a system of national development and security. But above all, perhaps, local administration is a response to demands from citizens for understandable and convenient government.

There are, of course, many organisational forms of this local administration in British government. There are local branches of central government departments (including jointly, as in the government offices of the regions), of public corporations (an endangered species), of special-purpose or *ad hoc* bodies (including the misnamed QUANGOS) such as the National Health Service and the administration of justice, and a myriad of local lay appointed bodies. And there are local authorities both directly and indirectly elected. In all this we may distinguish three broad types of local administration based on the nature of the relationship of government and the governed:

(a) *devolution*: local administration in which power and authority is delegated to statutory elected bodies;

(b) *decentralisation*: administrative arrangements in which services of national agencies are provided locally, and

(c) *deconcentration*: the physical dispersion of national government organisations throughout its territory.

Moreover, recent privatisations and related developments such as the private finance initiative remind us of a history of local public service provision through non-government organisations such as voluntary bodies and private companies, some, as in the public sector, indigenous to the locality, others being the local branches of national entities. Together these public and private organisations contribute local services in the often complex relationship that is British local governance. But how is local self-government justified within this relationship?

THE CONTRIBUTION OF LOCAL SELF-GOVERNMENT TO THE DEMOCRATIC STATE

W.J.M. Mackenzie commented on the centenary of John Stuart Mill's treatise on *Considerations on Representative Government* (1861) that 'There is no normative general theory from which we can deduce what local government ought to be; there is no positive general theory from which we can derive testable hypotheses about what it is. In fact the subject is a very base one' (1961/1975: 68). It will be clear from this volume that our current debate of democratic renewal in local government is the poorer for this condition (*pace* Stoker, 1996). Nevertheless, we can begin to distinguish local government from other forms of local administration and governance. Each authority is *multi-purpose*, allowing it to provide for the needs of its citizens in a comprehensive way, there is a *statutory basis* for the authority to raise revenue and make decisions in its own right and, perhaps most importantly for our purposes in this article, the legitimacy for its decisions lies in its appointment through *popular election*.

What then is the distinctive contribution of local self-government to the democratic state? Without a gross injustice to the subtleties of the different arguments in the philosophy of local self-government, we may distinguish between those theories which have argued that local self-government makes a functional contribution to the well-being of the democratic state and those which argue that, on the contrary, it is dysfunctional. Of the former, the classic orthodox exposition is to be found in Mill (1861: Chapter 15). He argued, first, that 'It is but a small portion of the public business of a country which can be well done, or safely attempted, by the central authorities' and that 'Not only are separate executive officers required for purely local duties ... but the popular control over those officers can only be advantageously exerted through a separate organ' (1861/1992: 376–7). Thus local government was regarded as necessary to the effective division of the labour of governing, the necessity being part administrative and part constitutional. But, more important still ('hardly any language is strong enough to represent the strength of my conviction' (378)) is the contribution that local self-government makes as 'the chief instrument' in the public education of the citizens. Thus, for Mill, local self-government enhanced the democratic state as a provider of local services, a counter to the central administration and a vehicle for political education.

In the early twentieth century the Webbs adapted and extended some of these ideas into a social democratic philosophy of local government (1920: part 2, chapter 4). They argued that local authorities could serve and champion working people against the national government and thus contribute to social progress directly. Moreover, local government could provide the arena in which local victories for socialism could be won. Municipalisation could be a prelude to nationalisation.

Although these social democratic ideas were not referred to explicitly by Mackenzie (1961/1975), his discussion encompassed a range of the functional arguments and argued that there had developed a 'blended orthodoxy' in support of local self-government: 'English local government is justified because it is a traditional institution. It is justified because it is an effective and convenient way to provide certain services. It is justified because we like to think that our central government needs the kind of qualities which are best trained by local self-government' (79–80).

Whether this blended orthodoxy sustains to this day is perhaps questionable. The period during which Mackenzie was writing was something of a golden time for local government. After the Second World War local authorities were very much the creature of the central government's programme of reconstruction and development. The financing of local authorities, for example, was dominated by specific grants and over most of England, at least, the nationalisation of local politics was completed by the emergence of local branches of national political parties contesting and assuming power in their authorities much as their national counterparts were doing at Westminster. However, the financial regime gradually relaxed during the 1950s and was symbolised by the Local Government Act of 1958 in which a plethora of direct and specific grants was replaced by a single block grant which gave local authorities more budgetary and therefore policy discretion. However, by the mid-1970s this party was pronounced well and truly over by Anthony Crosland, who, as Secretary of State for the Environment, warned a local government audience in, prophetically, the Free Trade Hall, Manchester, that local government spending in particular had to be kept within the country's ability to pay. This was the start of two decades in which central government saw local authorities increasingly as instruments of national policy.

This reining in of the discretion of local authorities and the inequalities which it engendered is no doubt welcomed by adherents of the 'dysfunctional' position, that is, those who argue that local self-government undermines the democratic state. If the 'functional' position of the blended orthodoxy sees local self-government as a form of mild democratic flavour enhancer, the dysfunctionalists see local self-government more as a free radical in the body politic with the potential to threaten its well-being. Histories of the theory of local self-government tend to see the dysfunctional argument as essentially a continental European idea. Certainly, it has strong continental exemplars. Rudolf Von Gneist, Professor of Law at the University of Berlin from the late 1850s and described by Poole (1979) as strangely attracted to the study of English local institutions, criticised the development of English local government in the nineteenth century as destroying liberty. The system would intensify the bureaucracy of government, undermine social stability and threaten both the paternalism and participation which so favourably characterised the British constitution. Thus, more local government meant more government, which in turn meant less liberty.

A second powerful strand in the dysfunctionalist school has more recent adherents as well as classic exemplars. Georges Langrod, a Polish national holding professorships at both Parisian and Brazilian universities, gave the seminal account of this argument in a paper to the International Political Science Association at the Hague in 1952 (subsequently published, Langrod, 1953). At the heart of the Langrod argument is an echo of Rousseau in the sense that local government competes against the will of the majority and seeks to inhibit the development of the social community by perpetuating inequality of area within the system:

> Democracy ... tends everywhere and at all times to create a social *whole*, a community which is uniform, levelled and subject to rules. ... On the other hand, local government is, by definition, a phenomenon of differentiation, of individualism, of separation. ... Democratisation of the state tends to transform its government progressively into a *self-government* of the whole population – which must, during the course of this evolution, make any local arrangement, 'opposed' to the central government, superfluous and devoid of any logical basis. (1953: 28–9, italics in original)

This argument is essentially, therefore, that local self-government undermines democratisation through inhibiting wholeness of political community and sustaining inequality of area. The reader does not have to be a victim of a local authority hegemony or an ally of a central government in the face of local intransigence to have sympathy with the broad thrust of this critique of local government even if the central concepts, equality of area and uniformity of system, seem closely related to both the original idea of city state in Rousseau and the immediate post-1945 context of eastern Europe. Moreover, in the notable symposium of discussion which followed Langrod's exposition in the pages of *Public Administration* (Panter-Brick, 1954; Moulin, 1954) and in later surveys in the 1960s and 1970s (for example, Mackenzie, 1961; Smith, 1969; Sharpe, 1970), there was wide recognition that local self-government was not a prerequisite for a democratic political system.

This brief review of arguments in the philosophy of local self-government demonstrates, first, that there was much more discussion of the justification of local self-government in the 1950s and 1960s than during the present reception of New Labour's proposals, second, that an inherent dilemma faces a British government seeking to manage democratic renewal and, third, that the justification for local self-government is neither self-evident nor universally accepted.

NEW LABOUR AND AN OLD DILEMMA

The current government faces, therefore, an old dilemma between the pursuit of a central government mandate for national uniformity and local mandates for differentiation. In a sense this dilemma may be expressed as a choice between the three types of local administration described above (devolution, decentralisation and deconcentration) and represented along a continuum in Figure 1. We have characterised the blended orthodoxy which has sustained local self-government for most of the past century as decentralisation tending to devolution. In a similar way, we have placed the functionalist theories of local self-government further towards the devolution end of the continuum and the dysfunctionalist theories towards the deconcentration end.

FIGURE 1

NEW LABOUR AND THE OLD DILEMMA

Devolution..........................Decentralisation...........................Deconcentration

     Λ   Λ   Λ

  Functionalist   Blended   Dysfunctionalist

  Theories   Orthodoxy   Theories

             < - - - - - - - New Labour? - - - - - - >

In determining its place along this continuum the government might have been expected to have addressed the concepts at the heart of the arguments. What, for example, are purely local services? To what extent is local self-government based upon a sense of community or local sources of finance? How far can local government act as a buffer to the central government? What are the mechanisms by which local self-government provides political education and training and what is the evidence of their success? What are the characteristics of the nationalisation of local politics and what are their effects on the independence of local authorities? Yet the consultative documents and White Paper (Cm. 4014, 1998) indicate a somewhat different set of questions: how can local democracy be renewed; how can participation in local government be enhanced; how can services provided by local authorities be made more responsive to local community needs? Although relevant and interesting, these questions reveal a partial view of local government's purpose, conduct and relations with its public, issues we return to below.

An intriguing echo can be heard here of the work of another Victorian functionalist theorist, Joshua Toulmin Smith. Writing in the 1840s and 1850s as only a man possessed could (this period included his famous battles with the centrist reformer Edwin Chadwick), Toulmin Smith found arguments for local self-government from within human nature (Toulmin Smith, 1849; see also Greenleaf, 1975). Thus local government reminded citizens to rely upon themselves rather than the national government, to realise the conditions in which they could enhance their personal liberties and above all to participate throughout the local administration. This was a doctrine which encouraged as local a form of self-government as possible and is echoed in New Labour's desire to see participation as part of a strengthened community governance (Cm. 4014, Chs. 4, 8).

Yet, what *is* Labour's philosophy of local self-government? One interpretation of the government's White Paper and other pronouncements would place it further towards the devolution end of the continuum in Figure 1 than even the blended orthodoxy. But this interpretation depends upon overlooking important tensions between government through local councillors and government through direct democracy (for example, by referendums and citizens' juries). Further, some elements of the government's proposals, for example the designation of and sanctions on 'failing councils' (not in themselves new, of course, as Poplar in the 1920s and Clay Cross in the 1960s can testify), appear to reinforce the role of local authorities as instruments of central government while simultaneously distancing the latter from any blame attached to the former's misdeeds. This places the government somewhere between the decentralisation and deconcentration end of the Figure 1 continuum.

To speculate rather less wildly on New Labour's programme for democratic renewal of local government requires a clearer expression of the government's meaning of local self-government than we are likely to receive, given the realities of government and politics. If New Labour has a coat of arms, its supporting motto is surely *what matters is what works*. This is perhaps an understandable pragmatic response to the doctrinal climate of the past two decades. Nevertheless, the history of local government suggests that its contexts have been varied and called for contingent responses rather than any absolute or universalist position. Thus, there are good grounds for expressing the motto more elaborately as 'what works for whom in what circumstances'. Yet the pragmatism cannot be sustained without some guiding principles or philosophy of local government. The remainder of this article seeks to tease out the government's position at least in terms of democratic renewal, the condition it is intended to remedy and potential effectiveness of the solutions.

DEMOCRATIC RENEWAL AND CONSTITUTIONAL REFORM: PARTICIPATION AND ALIENATION

The recognition that 'something needed to be done' about local government was identified by New Labour before it came to power in 1997. Indeed, the call for democratic renewal can be specifically linked to New Labour's programme for constitutional reform set out by Tony Blair several months before his election triumph (Blair, 1996: 33). For the then leader of the opposition, British politics had become characterised by low respect for both politicians and institutions, limited accountability and a remoteness of politics from most people's lives. To counteract this erosion of democracy and loss of political authority he proposed a programme of democratic or constitutional renewal: strengthening citizens rights and obligations, bringing decision making closer to people and improving representative and legislative systems.

In practical terms this programme for democratic renewal included a new notion of democratic citizenship and local government reform. That 'the revival of local government must be the prime means ... of taking government closer to the people' (Blair, 1997: 34) reflected an argument already put forward by Mandelson and Liddle (1996) in the most influential blueprint for New Labour's thinking in its first year in government. Advocating decentralisation together with the development of local and regional identity, Mandelson and Liddle called for the promotion of local democracy and 'the civil values and civic pride that go with the best of it'. They added that 'Labour understands that the best thing about local government is that it is local' (197).

Hence, proposals for the democratic renewal of local government emerge not in isolation, but as part of an agenda for new politics that seeks to *redefine* the relationship between the citizen and the state through the renovation of political institutions and processes at central and community levels. The watchwords include relevance, openness, trust and partnership. The intention is more than the simple changing of democratic practices or the tinkering with local government (and other institutions) in isolation. Rather, it is seen as a comprehensive reform strategy which, if taken literally, must involve the diffusion of power away from central government bodies to intermediate institutional and individuals, thus redefining *government* into a new system of *governance* (Stoker, 1996). Further, and importantly, reform is also designed to counteract what is seen to be mass withdrawal, if not *alienation*, from the political system in general and the local political system in particular.

Recent assessments of the state of UK politics and democracy have often focused on what is described as a state of alienation from political institutions and political participation. Beetham, for example, in exploring the democratic possibilities of local government, sees local self-government as a potential force to mitigate 'alienation from the political process on the part of significant parts of public opinion, and of whole localities'. Here alienation is linked to the development of quangos or appointed bodies which 'reinforce a conception of politics as the exclusive property of one party or section of opinion and its representativeness' (1996: 39). Such problems are often seen as the cause of low public expectations of local politics and a reluctance of citizens to turn out in local elections and otherwise participate in the representative process.

Such failures in participation have been explored by Stoker (1991; 1996) and others (Commission for Local Democracy, 1995; Pratchett and Wilson, 1996a) in terms of the perceived failures of traditional forms of local representative democracy and the possible growth of new political forms to rejuvenate it. Stoker, for example, asks whether involving people on the basis of direct material interest (for example, via school boards or housing management co-operatives) provides more effective mechanisms of representation than traditional representative forms (1996:17), and Pratchett and Wilson (1996a) suggest that failure to participate in democratic practices and institutions may be an endemic feature of twentieth century culture reflected in contradictions at local level. They cite survey evidence indicating that, while democracy is generally highly regarded, voters' principal concerns appear to be levels of local taxation and service efficiency rather than the loss of democratic accountability, the centralisation of local finances and the erosion of directly provided services.

The *alienated* voters (or perhaps better *abstainers*) are therefore also the *idle* (or *non-participatory*) rather than the *active* citizens. As such they represent the heathen that New Labour seeks to convert since, in the world of modernisation, idleness, if not a sin, does not elevate one to a state of grace. Further, in the political mind, the blame lies not at the centre of government but rather with a system of local government that has distanced itself from its electorate and conserved its powers. This has led to calls for the creation of local political structures that 'capture the imagination and enthusiasm of local people' (DETR, 1998: 1.8) and exhortations by ministers for an assault on voter apathy and political alienation (Armstrong, 1998).

Yet exactly what is this condition that the programme of 'democratic renewal' seeks to address? If it is indeed a state of alienation then perhaps we would benefit from exploring this concept in more detail in an effort identify whether it can be operationalised. To do this we turn inquisitively to the literature on alienation and specifically the ideas of Robert Blauner (1964).[1] For Blauner, alienation is a concept that can only be explained through sociological and social-psychological reasoning. More specifically, alienation should be seen as a 'quality of personal experience which results from specific types of social arrangements' (1964: 15). Consequently there exist relationships between social structure and behaviour which may increase or decrease alienation. Thus for Blauner the concept is multi-dimensional. Alienation exists when individuals are unable to control their immediate activities, develop a sense of purpose and function, belong to integrated communities, and when they fail to perceive activities as means of self-expression. This leads him to develop what he terms his four dimensions of alienation: (a) *powerlessness*, (b) *meaninglessness,* (c) *isolation* and (d) *self-estrangement.*[2]

Individuals are said to be *powerless* when they are controlled and manipulated by other persons or impersonal systems and when they cannot assert themselves to change or modify this situation: the powerless person reacts rather than acts and is directed rather than self-directed (Blauner, 1964: 16). Thus the opposite of powerlessness is *control. Meaninglessness*, in contrast, stems from the perception of a lack of purpose in an activity. Classically it is seen to relate to the nature and content of the activity itself and to the social context in which it is conducted. Efforts are seen as pointless if they fail to assist the achievement of personal goals or wider organisational or community objectives and energy applied to such activities will be minimised or withdrawn. Hence the opposite of meaninglessness is the perception of *purpose* and *function. Isolation* springs from no sense of belonging or a lack of identification with wider organisational systems and goals. In classical sociological terms this is often seen to stem from the absence of community in a meaningful sense or an identifiable organisational focus. The opposite of isolation is therefore *social integration*, although it should be noted that this can be realised in a variety of ways. *Self-estrangement* is seen as an individual who has become personally detached from activities rather than involved or engrossed in them. Such activities are often seen as an end in themselves rather than as a means to an end offering little in the way of opportunity for self-expression or initiative. The counter-factual to this is *self-involvement*, although as Blauner observes not all individuals may wish to become involved.[3] Hence, in these terms, alienation is most likely to be experienced by individuals when (a) they are powerless and lack control, (b) they see no purpose in their activities, and (c) they feel isolated from a network of community and personal relations (Blauner, 1964: 33). Yet alienation is not necessarily a malign condition. Rather, it may be an inevitable outcome of social, political and organisational changes in wider society. Hence a central question is less how to eliminate alienation than how to identify the situations that exacerbate and minimise it.

While the Blauner thesis may not be easily transferred from its original context to the democratic renewal debate, it at least provides a useful way to probe the concept of political alienation in greater detail. In particular it offers a framework for asking whether proposals for democratic renewal bring opportunities for increased control, a greater sense of purpose and an enhanced sense of involvement in terms of relations between citizens and local polities and, in a different way, between central and local government. We return to these necessary elements of a theory of local government in the final sections of this paper. First, however, we examine in more detail the ways in which New Labour's theoretical approach to constitutional reform and democratic renewal have been translated into practice both generally and, more specifically, in the context of local government.

DEMOCRATIC RENEWAL AND THE MODERNISATION OF LOCAL GOVERNMENT: FROM THEORY TO PRACTICE

The battle cry of New Labour has been the 'Third Way'. This 'modernising movement of the centre' (Giddens, 1998a) responds to challenges such as globalisation and changing patterns of social organisation by creating a knowledge-based economy built on individual empowerment and opportunity, a civil society enshrining rights and responsibilities and a modernised system of government based on partnership and decentralisation (Blair, 1998a; Giddens, 1998b). Its rhetoric can be found in the government's annual report (Cm 3969, 1998), the Health Service White Paper (Cm 3807, 1998), and the Local Government White Paper (Cm 4014, 1998). Yet while some commitments, notably to devolution to Scotland and Wales, have been delivered, other initiatives, such as open government and electoral reform, appear to have run into the sand. This may be rational in political terms but it also raises questions of the coherence of the modernisation agenda and the tensions underlying it.

Such tensions are evident in the government's programme for democratic renewal of local government. Its logic can be traced through Tony Blair's recent contribution to this debate (1998b), the government's consultative paper on local democracy and community leadership (DETR, 1998), the White Paper itself (Cm 4014, 1998) and efforts to market the proposals to local authorities (Stoker, 1998). In Blair's view there are three main reasons for modernising local government: (1) local government has lost a sense of direction, (2) there is a lack of coherence and integration in service delivery and (3) the quality of local services is too variable (Blair, 1998b: 10–13). This analysis, developed in more detail in the consultative paper, is stronger on prescription than providing evidence to support the claims being made and assumes that low interest and participation in local government and local politics are indeed the product of these qualities.

For Blair, modern local government requires a new democratic legitimacy, new ways of working, new disciplines and new powers (1998b: 10–12). The need for democratic legitimacy is linked to low electoral turnout and low participation in local political life. The search for new ways of working is based on the failure of traditional ways of doing business in local government and the complexity and inefficiency of complex structures. The call for new disciplines arises from a failure of local government to promote quality in service delivery and, at times, conduct itself according to the highest ethical standards. Finally, the search for new powers is linked to a vision of a role for local government as a partner in a wider network of local organisations rather than the sole or principal service provider for a locality (Blair, 1998b; DETR, 1998; Cm 4014, 1998). The Third Way for local government is therefore predicated on it finding a 'new role for a new millennium' (Blair, 1998b: 13). This involves developing a local vision, providing a focus for partnership and guaranteeing quality services. The practical solutions for modernising local government therefore take a number of forms: (a) modernising leadership, (b) democratisation, (c) promoting community well-being and (d) enhancing quality and effectiveness.

Providing leadership is a central theme on the government's agenda. Local government needs 'recognised leaders to fulfil the community leadership role' (Blair, 1998b: 16). To this end the government proposals include elected mayors with significant powers, executive-led local councils and a separation of councillor executive and representative roles (DETR, 1998: Ch.5; Cm 4014: Ch.3). Solutions for further democratisation include encouraging local authorities to experiment with differing modes of participation (consultation, citizens' juries, surveys, focus groups and so on), improving systems for voter registration and voting arrangements and seeking ways to make active political representation more accessible and attractive to a wider variety of individuals and (DETR, 1998: Ch.3; Cm 4014: Ch.4).

Creating community well-being will involve both the imposition of statutory responsibilities on local government to promote the social, economic and environmental well-being of their areas and encouragement for them to enter into partnerships with other organisations (Cm 4014: Ch.8). This focus is seen by some as central to the government's concept of local self-government. Indeed, Stoker argues that this 'includes a commitment to developing techniques to encourage the alienated, socially excluded and the disadvantaged to participate' (1998: 10), which, in the spirit of Mill, he links to enhanced citizen education supported by a strategic use of information technologies to provide a new infrastructure for participation. And with all this goes the requirement for local government to pursue quality and efficiency through 'best value' which will impose a duty on councils to deliver services to a clear standard by the most efficient, economic and effective means available. Through it councils will be able to demonstrate their strategic effectiveness as well as their credentials for leading local partnerships (Cm 4014: Ch.7).

This is undoubtedly a wide-ranging and ambitious agenda. To assess the extent to which it addresses the core questions of democratic renewal we turn to three issues central to the idea of local self-government raised above and explored here as: (a) the empowerment of local authorities and citizens, (b) the meaning of local government to political actors and citizens and (c) the encapsulation of community identities in local authorities.

In response to the government's consultative proposals for enhancing participation at local elections, the Local Government Association argued that: 'It is clear to us that low turnout is not a local government problem. We believe that participation in local government elections is linked to voter perceptions of whether or not it is worth voting – whether the local authority has the ability to "make a difference" within its locality' (1998: 3.25). This is, of course, a classical problem of political science calling on theories of voting behaviour and interest groups as well as, more broadly, public choice (Dowding, 1996). It also raises wider issues of participation (other than voting) and engagement in the practice of local politics (for example, why be a councillor). These are questions of behaviour and motivation linked inevitably to personal goals, values and incentive structures. Hence, in terms of the discussion of alienation above, part of the answer relates to the relative power of actors to control their situation. If local authorities have little real power, why bother to participate either as a prospective representative or voter? In a different way, should participation initiatives be judged in terms of the control they give individuals, that is, are they genuine vehicles for empowerment? Now this is tricky territory, not least since empowerment can be interpreted in a variety of ways (Cochrane, 1996). However, one should be cautious of current initiatives (Cm 4014, 1996) that seek to promote democratic renewal almost as a *precondition* for the yielding of greater powers. This is to ignore what Beetham (1996) terms the vicious circle of accountability and representation *vis-à-vis* citizen involvement and participation. This can only be broken by reform from two directions simultaneously – increasing local government autonomy and allowing it to offer more imaginative policy choices by giving it greater control and hence greater salience for those who are directly involved and engage with it.

Yet salience is related to meaning and purpose. The democratic renewal debate, as articulated by the government, undoubtedly seeks to engage local authorities with the public in a more systemised manner and also to make local government more relevant. Can these proposals succeed? As Pratchett and Wilson (1996b) note, surveys from Widdicombe (1986) onwards indicate that traditionally the public has low knowledge of local government's functions and operations. To this can be added a declining faith in the ability of local government to influence local affairs (Rao, 1993, 1998; Young and Rao, 1995). Offering results from the British Social Attitudes Survey, Young and Rao caution against blanket judgements in that responses on the salience and effectiveness of local government clearly vary with age and situation. However, caveats aside, what seems clear is that local government has become a world of contradictions reflected, for example, in the willingness of voters to follow party lines at the ballot box but in the expectation that those elected will pursue a locality's interests once elected (Rao, 1998). Evidence from these studies also indicates the difficulties of recruiting and retaining councillors: the reluctance to stand in the first instance and the rapid turnover of many who are elected, often as a result of experience failing to match expectations (Bloch, 1992; Rao, 1993).

Hence the essence of minimising alienation is the introduction of a sense of purpose and function. Proposals for democratic renewal need to be judged in terms of whether they are likely to provide and enhance these both in terms of local political representation (the recruitment and retention of members) and the engagement of citizens themselves. In these terms writers such as Stoker (1998) may be optimistic in claiming that the government's commitment to community governance and its leadership, as set out in the White Paper and consultative documents, will address the problem. Rather the reforms may enhance patterns of participation by those already included but fail to engage the alienated. In the Blauner typology, for example, alienation is intensified by a sense of isolation and mitigated by mechanisms for social integration. In the wider world of politics this might lead to an examination of 'exclusion' in terms of those who see themselves as outside the political process completely as well as those who may participate but still feel unable to relate to a larger system. One must tread carefully here. One cannot assume that all those excluded wish to be included and there is a further danger in perceiving community and locality as identical (Frazer, 1996). Indeed, as Beetham argues, the question of what is political space is a central puzzle in our changing world: 'the formal political sphere is defined as a bounded territory, which may or may not (in the UK usually *not*) correspond to any coherent geographical entity with which people can identify. The informal political sphere, on the other hand, is now a potentially boundless space' (1996: 47; italics in original).

In practical terms this puzzle was encountered by the Local Government Commission for England (Banham Commission) in its (perhaps misguided) search to establish community identity. Yet what *is* local? And, in terms of social integration, is one seeking a revitalised system of local representative democracy in the traditional sense or some wider conception of local democracy as hinted at by Beetham above? In the White Paper, John Prescott calls for a fundamental shift of culture involving a radical refocusing of local authorities' traditional roles (Cm 4014, 1998: 4). But in terms of social integration is what is proposed radical enough? In its final report the Commission for Local Democracy (CLD) set out a much more proactive agenda with proposals for citizen education, wide-ranging consultation mechanisms including referenda and a local democracy plan to keep a check on initiatives for decentralisation and citizen involvement (Commission for Local Democracy, 1995: Ch.5). As Pratchett and Wilson observe, such suggestions, disarmingly simple at first glance, may hide a subversively radical agenda: 'Beneath the surface, however, their implications are profound because they aim to change and influence the underlying attitudes and culture of citizens, to encourage them to become more politically aware and active and to make government more responsive' (1996b: 242).

In part, the government's current proposals (Cm 4014, 1998: Ch.4) take up a number of the CLD's suggestions (for example, local referenda) yet the latter's programme offers a more far-reaching programme for cultural change towards an active citizenry, a development that, while facilitating social integration, would generate disruptive waves in the world of both local and national politics. Thus this also reveals tensions and dilemmas which have to be addressed in the democratic renewal of local government. And it is to these that we turn in our conclusion.

CONCLUSION: STRENGTHENING A FRAGILE DEMOCRACY?

Hilary Armstrong, stewardess of best value, has been one of the most active and public of junior ministers in the new Labour government. Unlike some of her colleagues, she has not been afraid of speaking to all sorts of gatherings, including academic. At one such occasion, the Political Studies Association (Public Administration Group) seminar at which some of the papers in this volume were first presented, she commented on a number of the challenges facing the government's programme of democratic renewal of local government. She suggested, for example, that 'local democracy is very fragile in the British system of government'. Reinforcing local government's position was at the forefront of the government's programme of democratic renewal. But she warned that the experience of the poll tax had inhibited major reform of local government in general as well as local finance in particular. Thus progress had to be measured and proportionate. But no one was to doubt the government's intentions.

Is local government so fragile? Will the government's reforms provide for the requisite renewal of local self-government? How far do they reflect traditional ways of regarding local government in this country and how far do they represent a new order? Our aim in this article has been to provide a conceptual discussion to inform the answer to these questions and to assess the extent to which current ideas for democratic renewal in local government represent theoretical and constitutional *continuity or change* in the British democratic tradition. We may conclude that there is certainly continuity in the government's proposals with the traditions of local government. Indeed, in many respects the programme seems to represent a tinkering with the products of the 'blended orthodoxy' identified by Mackenzie (1961/1975) and discussed above. Yet there is the potential for radical change, to break from this orthodoxy and alter radically the contribution of local self-government to the British political system. This requires, however, a more explicit recognition than hitherto of the tensions and dilemmas inherent within a democratic state which espouses local self-government.

This paper has suggested that these tensions are between (1) the integrating mandate of the unitary state and the differentiating mandates of local self-government, (2) the electoral representative process and direct democracy, and (3) enactment through legislation which commands democratic renewal or through a commitment to of a common set of values which is used to guide conduct throughout the polity. The first of these, the integration–differentiation tension, is a classic policy dilemma. As Hood reminded us (1975), dilemmas cannot be managed effectively by tinkering. They represent mutually exclusive objectives and values. They may be resolved only for a particular period of time by identifying the priorities inherent in the choice. This is particularly pertinent to the government's problem. It has to ask itself what is the condition within the British political system (note, not just within local government) that needs addressing. If it is that the state has become too centrist to deal flexibly and responsively with the demands of its citizens and of rapidly changing economic and social environments, then it may determine that the values which need to be promoted are those of redressing this imbalance for our time by extending the devolution of power beyond Scotland and Wales through English regions and into localities, thereby enhancing the plural government of differentiated local areas and accepting the likely consequential increased variability. If, on the other hand, the priority is developmental, perhaps similar in aim to the period after the Second World War, with common national policies and values at its heart, then the government may determine a regime in which the discretion of local authorities is further limited as they fulfil a role more akin to agencies of the national government.

The government would wish, as do we all, to have it both ways – 'responsiveness to local differentiation' and 'consistency of service across the country' (as Armstrong pronounced at the PSA seminar). This would suggest that the government's approach is based not on managing a choice between alternative values (which is what confronts it) but tinkering with apparatus. What is clear from our discussion is that this is also bound to produce an unsatisfactory outcome: ineffective services and intensified alienation. Moreover, it is doubtful if the government can rejuvenate the internal democratic vitality of local government while diminishing its devolutionary quotient.

Assuming that New Labour does wish to enhance the devolutionary quotient, it will then face a second tension, that between the competing claims of representative apparatus and particularly between electoral and extra-electoral mechanisms. Thus far, government documentation has made much of its intentions to enhance the opportunities and overall levels of participation in local government, but has not, it seems, recognised the tension (including competing mandates) that might ensue for electoral representation. Local authorities are traditionally appointed by and accountable through popular election. Thus, for some, democratic renewal is less about extra-electoral participation than enhancing the representative qualities of the electoral process. Intriguingly, this argument is often used in the current debate by those in essentially one-party authorities to protect their positions. Yet this approach opens up the very real prospect of electoral reform to effect representative qualities – reforms which are indeed likely to undermine party hegemony. For some this would be a real gain in the purpose and function of elections and encourage involvement. Even if this tension between the electoral and extra-electoral mechanisms of local democracy may not be a policy dilemma (mutually exclusive objectives), it still requires a clear vision of the values to be promoted and the management of consequential effects of changes to them.

Finally, there is to be resolved the choice of reform enactment. There is a tendency for new administrations to wish to flex their legislative muscles, to rely on governance by command. Gradually they learn that legislation may provide a framework but cannot resolve problems without a set of values shared with policy implementers. So much of the life of our political institutions is shaped not by the organisation of structure and process but by the commitments and relationships of those who work them, that is, a communion mode of governance which can facilitate the reduction of alienation. In this reality lies the greatest continuity with our past but also the potential for change in the future.

For the present, however, while there is considerable discussion about the future of local government, a matter remarkable in itself, these tensions do not seem to be widely recognised nor at the heart of the government's thinking despite its explicit attempt to put forward community as a resolving concept. The prospect, it must be admitted, is for a fudged orthodoxy to evolve as the product of pragmatic responses which have overlooked fundamental tensions in the philosophy of local government and the complex causes underlying participation in local political life. In some ways we are back with Toulmin Smith and Chadwick in the middle of the nineteenth century as we tussle with the centrist and localist forces. Perhaps we need to recall another nineteenth-century figure: 'The necessity for external government to man is in an inverse ratio to the vigour of his self-government' (Coleridge, 1851).

NOTES

1. In classical terms the concept of alienation is firmly rooted in Marxist theory although, as Blauner notes, later developments have seen the term widened and applied to a wide range of situations and circumstances some way from its original conceptualisation (1964: Ch.1). Blauner's own concerns are with the alienation of workers in the labour process and the effect of various developments such as changing circumstances in the external and internal environment of work, in particular technology, on this. As such his methodology and analysis have met with criticisms from later writers in this area (for example, Salaman, 1981; Thompson, 1984). While this debate is important and significant we do not see it as central here where our purpose in using Blauner is in an effort to widen the discussion of political alienation.

2. Blauner's intention is to develop a multi-dimensional rather than a unitary conception of alienation. In doing this he draws heavily on earlier work by Seeman (1959) that seeks to identify various ways alienation has been conceptualised in social theory. Blauner confesses to a 'free' adaptation of Seeman's ideas and similarly here we rather freely transfer Blauner to the political context. However, we would argue that doing so offers the opportunity to widen the debate on political alienation that is often tied rather narrowly to behaviouralist debates on political participation and voting behaviour (see, for example, Dowse & Hughes, 1986, Ch.10; Orum, 1989: Ch.9).

3. There is a danger in assuming that individuals are naturally seeking community or wish to participate actively in social and political life. Values and goals may be achieved in a variety of ways and indeed as Beetham (1996) and, more extremely Mulgan (1994) suggest, individuals and groups may now often reject traditional political practices and institutions for alternative forms to achieve their goals. If this is the case then traditional institutions and processes may be unable to meet individuals needs without radical structural and processual reforms.

REFERENCES

Armstrong, H., 1998, Speech to Local Government Association Conference, 8 July.
Beetham, D., 1996, 'Theorising Local Democracy and Local Government', in King and Stoker, 1996, pp.28–49.
Blair, T., 1996, 'Democracy's Second Age', *The Economist*, 14 Sept., pp.33–6.
Blair, T., 1998a, *The Third Way: New Politics for the New Century* (London: Fabian Society).
Blair, T., 1998b, *Leading the Way: A New Vision for Local Government* (London: Institute of Public Policy Research).
Blauner, R., 1964, *Alienation and Freedom* (Chicago, IL: University of Chicago Press).

Bloch, A., 1992, *The Turnover of Local Councillors* (York: Joseph Rowntree Foundation).

Cm 3807, 1997, *The New NHS: Modern, Dependable* (London: Stationery Office Ltd).

Cm 3969, 1998, *The Government's Annual Report 1997/8* (London: Stationery Office Ltd).

Cm 4014, 1998, *Modern Local Government: In Touch with the People* (London: Stationery Office Ltd).

Cochrane, A., 1996, 'From Theories to Practices: Looking for Local Democracy in Britain', in King and Stoker, 1996, pp.193–213.

Coleridge, S.T., 1851, *Coleridge's Table Talk*, entry for 15 June 1833, ed. H.N.C. (London: John Murray).

Commission for Local Democracy, 1995, *Taking Charge: The Rebirth of Local Democracy* (London: Municipal Journal Books).

Department of the Environment Transport and the Regions (DETR), 1998, *Modernising Local Government: Local Democracy and Community Leadership*, Consultation Paper (London: DETR), January.

Dowding, K., 1996, 'Public Choice and Local Governance', in King and Stoker, 1996, pp.50–66.

Dowse, R.E. and J.A. Hughes, 1986, *Political Sociology* (Chichester: John Wiley).

Frazer, E., 1996, 'The Value of Locality', in King and Stoker, 1996, pp.89–110.

Giddens, A., 1998a, 'After the Left's Paralysis', *New Statesman*, 1 May.

Giddens, A., 1998b, *The Third Way: The Renewal of Social Democracy* (London: Polity Press).

Gray, A.G. and W.I. Jenkins, 1998, 'New Labour, New Government? Change and Continuity in Public Administration and Government 1996–7', *Parliamentary Affairs*, Vol.51, No.2, pp.111–30.

Gray, A.G. and W.I. Jenkins, 1999, 'Modernisation and Democratisation? Developments in British Government and Administration 1997–8', *Parliamentary Affairs*, Vol.52, No.2, pp.139–60.

Greenleaf, W.H., 1975, 'Toulmin Smith and the British Political Tradition', *Public Administration*, Vol.53, No.1, pp.25–44.

Hood, C., 1975, *The Limits of Administration* (London: John Wiley).

King, D. and G. Stoker (eds.), 1996, *Rethinking Local Democracy* (London: Macmillan).

Langrod, G., 1953, 'Local Government and Democracy', *Public Administration*, Vol.31, No.1, pp.25–34.

Local Government Association (LGA), 1998, *Modernising Local Government: Local Government and Community Leadership: LGA Response to DETR Consultation Paper*, LGA, April.

Mackenzie, W.J.M., 1961/1975, *Theories of Local Government*, Greater London Paper No. 2, London School of Economics 1961 and reprinted in the version cited here: *Explorations in Government, Collected Papers 1951–68* (London: Macmillan, 1975).

Mandelson, P. and R. Liddle, 1996, *The Blair Revolution* (London: Faber & Faber).

Mill, J.S., 1861/1992, *Considerations on Representative Government*, 1861, and reprinted in the version cited here: H.B. Acton (ed.), *John Stuart Mill: Utilitarianism, On Liberty, Considerations on Representative Government* (London: Dent (Everyman's Library), 1992).

Moulin, L., 1954, 'Local Government as a Basis for Democracy: A Further Comment', *Public Administration*, Vol.32, No.4, pp.433–7.

Mulgan, G., 1994, *Politics in an Antipolitical Age* (London: Polity Press).

Orum, A.M., 1989, *Introduction to Political Sociology* (New Jersey: Prentice Hall).

Panter-Brick, K., 1954, 'Local Government and Democracy – A Rejoinder', *Public Administration*, Vol.31, No.4, pp.344–8.

Poole, K.P., 1979, 'The Values of Local Democracy', *Local Government Review*, 13 Jan., Vol.143, pp.17–19 and 26.

Pratchett, L. and D. Wilson, 1996a, 'Local Government under Siege', in L. Pratchett and D. Wilson (eds.), *Local Democracy and Local Government* (London: Macmillan), pp.1–19.

Pratchett, L. and D. Wilson, 1996b, 'What Future for Local Democracy?', in L Pratchett and D. Wilson (eds.), *Local Democracy and Local Government* (London: Macmillan), pp.229–49.

Rao, N., 1993, *Managing Change: Councillors and the New Local Government* (York: Joseph Rowntree Foundation).

Rao, N., 1998, 'Representation in Local Politics: A Reconsideration and Some New Evidence', *Political Studies*, 46, pp.19–35.

Salaman, G., 1981, *Class and Corporation* (Glasgow: Fontana).

Seeman, M. 1959, 'On the Meaning of Alienation', *American Sociological Review*, 24, pp.783–91.

Sharpe, L.J., 1970, 'Theories and Values of Local Government', *Political Studies*, Vol.18, No.2, pp.153–74.

Smith, B.C., 1969, 'The Justification of Local Government', in L.D. Edelman and M.D. Goldrick (eds.), *The Politics and Government of Urban Canada* (London: Methuen).

Stoker, G., 1991, *The Politics of Local Government* (2nd edn., London: Macmillan).

Stoker, G., 1996, 'Introduction: Normative Theories of Local Government and Democracy', in D. King and G. Stoker (eds.), *Rethinking Local Democracy* (London: Macmillan), pp.1–27

Stoker, G., 1998, *Democratic Renewal: Issues for Local Government* (London: Local Government Management Board).

Thompson, P., 1984, *The Nature of Work* (London: Macmillan).

Toulmin Smith, J., 1849, *Government by Commissions Illegal and Pernicious* (London: Sweet).

Webb, B. and S., 1920, *A Constitution for a Socialist Commonwealth of Great Britain* (London: Longmans, Green & Co.).

Widdicombe, D., 1986, *Report of Committee of Inquiry into Local Authority Business* (London: HMSO, Cmnd 9797).

Young, K. and N. Rao, 1995, 'Faith in Local Democracy', in R. Jowell *et al.*, *British Social Attitudes: 12th Report* (Aldershot: Gower), pp.92–117.

Public Participation and the Democratic Renewal Agenda: Prioritisation or Marginalisation?

STEVE LEACH AND MELVIN WINGFIELD

THE DEMOCRATIC RENEWAL AGENDA: JOINED UP OR FRAGMENTED?

The White Paper *Modern Local Government: In Touch with the People* (DETR, 1998) contains a range of proposals for modernising British local government. Some are concerned with improving the quality, cost-effectiveness and responsiveness of local services, in a project labelled 'Best Value', which will form the main content of the Local Government Bill, to be published and enacted during the 1998–99 parliamentary session. Other proposals, however, are concerned with the constitutional position of local government, which for various reasons is viewed as in need of 'democratic renewal'. There are four key elements to the democratic renewal programme: a set of proposals focused on improving electoral turnout in local elections; a commitment and proposed legislative framework for facilitating community leadership; a set of proposals for transforming the internal political management structures and processes of local authorities (centred on the idea of an executive/assembly split); and guidelines aimed at developing opportunities for citizens to participate in local government.

The public participation proposals are so far the least prescriptive of the elements in the government's modernisation programme for local government. But they are arguably the most fundamental. If the main aim is to re-establish local government in the hearts and minds of local people (as is frequently implied by Hilary Armstrong's speeches) then public participation has a much greater potential contribution to make than simply the introduction of new political management structures. The seriousness of the government's intentions are illustrated at various points in the White Paper, namely:

> New structures alone will not bring about renewal of local democracy
> ... that can only come about if there is ... close and regular contact

Steve Leach and Melvin Wingfield, De Montfort University

between a council and local people between elections (para. 4.1)
The Government wishes to see consultation and participation embedded in the culture of all councils ... and undertaken across a wide range of each council's responsibilities (para. 4.6).

However, there is some ambiguity about how far up the ladder of citizen participation (Arnstein, 1971) the government is advocating local authorities should go. As Arnstein shows, there is a world of difference between different forms of so-called citizen participation, which may range from tokenism, through information provision and consultation, to shared or delegated power over certain decisions. Although the use of the term 'citizen' in the White Paper rather than 'customer' or 'consumer' implies an expectation of direct public involvement in decision making, at other points it appears that the main emphasis is on service provision. Public participation should 'ensure that local authorities are reflecting the priorities and wishes of the people they serve' (para. 4.1). This sounds very much like an exhortation to improve responsiveness rather than the introduction of alternative structures of democracy.

If there is an ambiguity over what the government means by 'enhanced public participation', there is also an open-mindedness, much appreciated by local authorities, about how they should respond to this apparent priority. The White Paper contains the following passage:

The Government propose to legislate for a new statutory duty on councils to consult and engage with their local communities on these issues (community plan, local performance plan). Every council will have to decide which methods are the most appropriate in their own particular circumstances. Government does not propose to specify the form such consultation should take ... The way in which councils conduct consultation will be one of the issues taken into account in assessing how far a local authority is meeting its "best value" duty ... or is fit to be a "beacon council".

The implication of this passage is that local authorities will be *required* to do very little, apart from demonstrating that they are doing *something*. There is the potential 'stick' of sanctions for those authorities whose failure to provide 'best value' can be related to their lack of customer consultation (though here we are talking about familiar and widely accepted aspects of consultation such as MORI surveys and user group forums). There is the potential carrot that imaginative approaches to consultation may help to strengthen a case for 'beacon' status. But the opportunity is there for authorities who do not accept the importance of the public participation element in the DETR's agenda to marginalise it or pay lip service to it in developing programmes of change.

It is from the interviews in the case studies carried out in connection with the research[2] that we need to turn to gain an understanding of the political considerations which underpin the volume and pattern of adoption

Despite the verbal commitments of government ministers, the participation element of the democratic renewal agenda has yet to be embodied in legislation. 'Best Value' dominates the content of the Local Government Bill (1998). Arrangements for beacon council awards are already in hand. New political management structures and strengthened ethical standards provide most of the content of the draft Local Government (Organisation and Standards) Bill 1999, which includes nothing specific on new measures for public participation (see also DETR, 1999). Given this, failure to follow up the priority accorded to public participation in the White Paper, local authorities might be forgiven for putting participatory developments on hold. After all, there is much else that they are required to do.

There is thus, we would argue, both a lack of clarity in the White Paper about how the term 'participation' is to be interpreted, and plenty of scope in the legislative arrangement proposed for local authorities to prioritise or marginalise it. In fact, the ambiguity in the White Paper goes much further than this. In our view, a number of tensions – in some cases contradictions – can be identified between different elements of the White Paper. It is arguably less 'joined-up' than some of its protagonists think. If our interpretation is correct, the implication is that local authorities will have to make choices amongst different White Paper priorities – not absolute choices necessarily, but certainly choices of emphasis. As we demonstrate later in the article, both the proposals for new political management structures and the Best Value guidelines may if interpreted in certain ways limit the scope for enhanced public participation. In addition as our research[1] shows (Lowndes *et al.*, 1998a) there are a number of tensions and contradictions, and the related need for choices within the participation agenda itself. But first let us consider the current record of local authorities in relation to participation.

PUBLIC PARTICIPATION: THE RESEARCH FINDINGS

Many local authorities could and no doubt would argue, with some justification, that they have been for the past seven or eight years making the running in relation to public participation, and that, in large part, the participation agenda set out in the White Paper reflects what local authorities have already been doing. Certainly, the range of participation techniques referred to in the White Paper (such as visioning exercises,

FIGURE 1
CURRENT AND PLANNED USE OF FORMS OF PUBLIC PARTICIPATION

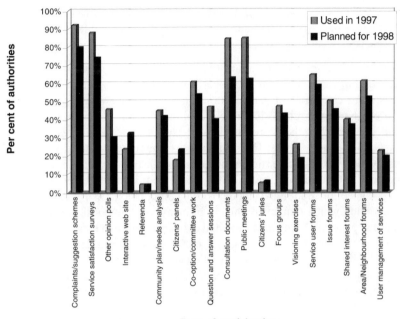

different forms of public participation and illustrates the extent to which public participation in local decision-making is clearly of growing interest for local authorities. While different authorities may apply different methods, there is a wide range of methods adopted by authorities.

However, it is possible to get beneath the service of this general trend by developing a categorisation of participation initiative. In the research we found it helpful to distinguish between four such categories of public participation:

- those which are essentially *traditional* in their format (for example, public meetings, consultation documents, co-option to committees and question and answer sessions);

- those which are primarily *customer oriented* in their purpose (for example, complaints/suggestion schemes, service satisfaction surveys and other opinion polls);

- *innovative methods* which are designed to *consult* citizens on particular issues (for example, interactive web-sites, citizens' panels, focus groups and referendums);

- *innovative methods* which seek to encourage greater citizen *deliberation* over issues (for example, citizens' juries, community plans/needs analysis, visioning exercises and issue forums).

The growth in the use of each of these is illustrated in Figures 2–5. Three key findings emerge from a comparison of the developments in each of these four categories of participation. First there is a contrast between, on the one hand, the relatively straight evolutionary lines of Figures 2 and 3, and on the other the more accelerated curves seen in Figures 4 and 5, especially since 1994. This emphasises the extent and diversity of innovation in public participation over the last few years. Second, the gradual but sustained growth in Figures 2 and 3 points to the continued importance of traditional methods of participation, and the customer orientation which remains dominant in many local authorities. Despite the rapid expansion of innovative methods of participation in local government, such initiatives still lag far behind conventional consultation processes. Finally, innovations in public participation are equally split between consultative and deliberative mechanisms. Indeed, it appears that the two categories complement one another in the process of democratic renewal.

FIGURE 2
TRENDS IN TRADITIONAL METHODS OF PUBLIC PARTICIPATION

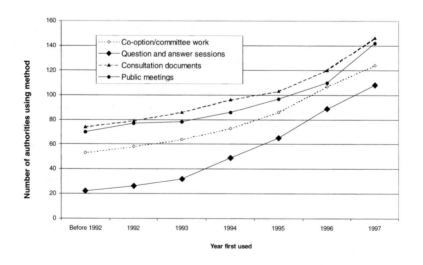

FIGURE 3
TRENDS IN CUSTOMER-ORIENTED CONSULTATION

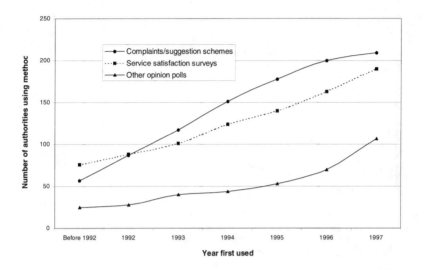

FIGURE 4
TRENDS IN INNOVATIVE METHODS

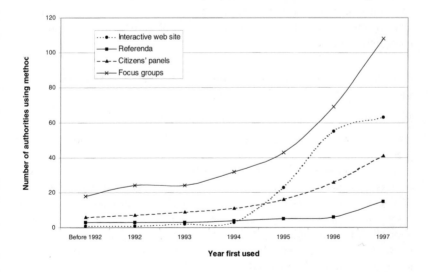

FIGURE 5
TRENDS IN INNOVATIVE METHODS OF DELIBERATION/PARTICIPATION

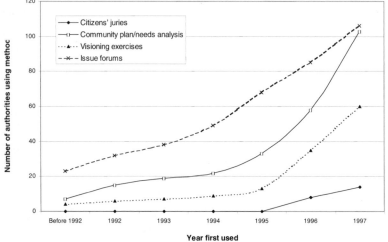

It is from the interviews in the case studies carried out in connection with the research[2] that we need to turn to gain an understanding of the political considerations which underpin the volume and pattern of adoption of different forms of public participation. This process will take us right back into the tensions and contradictions, which can be discerned at the heart of the White Paper. Four such tensions of particular significance are identified and discussed below.

POLITICAL PERCEPTIONS OF THE PARTICIPATORY AGENDA: TENSIONS AND CONTRADICTIONS

Representative Democracy and Participatory Democracy

One of the most significant findings of the case study research was the predominantly *informal* and *ad hoc* nature of the public participation strategies, which we came across in the case studies. There is a good reason for this. Enhanced public participation implies an injection of *participatory* democracy into the local body politic. John Stewart has argued that many forms of participatory democracy are compatible with and can indeed *strengthen* the institution of representative democracy, rather than weaken it. But this is not the way things are perceived, at least amongst the older and more traditionally inclined Labour and Conservative local councillors.

Even in one-party (local) states, where one of the normal conditions of representative democracy – the presence of a significant opposition – is lacking, there is no guarantee that the dominant party (at present typically Labour) will perceive the need for a more participatory approach.

However, even in local authorities still dominated by traditional Labour, there is typically a difference of emphasis between the council leader (and one or two of his or her closest associates) and the rank and file of the Labour group. The former recognises the reality of the 'democratic renewal' agenda of the Labour government, and its determination to introduce it, if necessary by prescription. In some cases that awareness co-exists with a genuine personal commitment to enhanced public participation, or at least some forms of it. In others it does not. The rank and file, however, are more likely to feel threatened by the new emphasis on public participation, and to argue from a variety of (often unconvincing) premises that representative democracy is in itself an adequate democratic institution.

Thus, in several of the case studies we listened to leaders explaining the necessity of a 'softly-softly' approach. Yes, he (or she) saw the need for a public participation strategy. But there was no way 'the group' would accept it yet. The leader's aim was to introduce public participation measures on an *ad hoc* basis, exploiting opportunities (for example, the rules of the game in relation to City Challenge and SRB bids) and gradually building up momentum. *Then*, in a year or so, by process of accretion, a commitment to public participation, evidenced by a wide range of examples, would have become apparent and it would become possible to switch from an informal (implicit) strategy, to a formal (explicit) one.

The interviews were carried out at a time when the LGA was urging the government to follow the example of the Hunt Committee in encouraging and facilitating voluntary experimentation with new forms of political management structure, rather than introducing prescriptive legislation on this topic. There was a perception that the demonstration of a readiness to innovate in other related areas of the democratic renewal agenda – for example, public participation – might contribute towards that desired outcome. Now that it has become clear that cabinet and or mayoral forms of government are to become *requirements*, there is a danger that public participation – where the legislation is likely, as we have seen, to be much less prescriptive, may fade into the background. Certainly the political and organisational energies of local authorities are currently (January 1999) being dominated by new political management structures and Best Value.

There is a corollary to this 'tension in principle' between representative democracy and participatory democracy. As much recent work shows (Young and Davies, 1990; Game and Leach, 1995; Copus, 1998), in all three major parties, the party group plays a fundamental role in deciding what the public stance of the party will be on all major issues (and in many cases, many minor issues as well) which are considered by council or committee. Interpretation of 'group discipline' varies, from highly formalised in most Labour groups, to relatively informal in most Liberal Democrat groups. But in most local authorities, most of the time, the content of what party group representatives (for example, committee chairs) say in public arenas has been largely predetermined at a group meeting of one form or another, as has the way the group will vote. Anything that threatens the authority of the group is invariably suspect! And public participation, particularly if the results of it are seen as binding (as in a binding referendum or the devolution of power to a neighbourhood forum) is clearly one such threat. Thus, as well as the general unease about 'participatory' democratic ideologies, there is the more specific tension between the party group as the main determinant of political stance (and, for a majority group, decision) and any interpretation of public participation which undermines that authority. Even consultative (non-binding) forms of participation may generate differences of view which have to be 'taken into account' in any public decision not to follow its recommendations.[3] From this perspective, the public participation agenda is potentially more threatening than cabinets and elected mayors, which are at least premised on familiar assumptions about the primacy of representative democracy.

Cabinet Government and Public Participation

The current committee system, for all its (many) limitations does have the advantage that every decision the authority makes (unless delegated to officers) appears on a public agenda with a background report (often leading to a recommendation) and is subject to a public debate. Of course many such decisions actually generate little or no public debate; but if there is an issue which has raised public concern, then that concern will almost certainly be expressed, either because back-bench or opposition councillors have picked it up, or because members of the public are allowed to appear and state their views at committee (most common at planning committees). This is not public participation in the terms discussed in the White Paper; but it is at least an opportunity for the public to challenge a decision before it is made.

Under cabinet government, whether or not it involves an elected mayor, many executive decisions which would previously have been made in public by a committee would become the subject of executive action, decided at a private meeting of the cabinet. It is true that lists of such decisions would have to be issued and it is likely that the power of scrutiny will involve, *inter alia*, the opportunity to refer contentious executive decisions to the assembly for public discussion before they are ratified. But this would necessarily be a selective process; referral would be the exception, not the norm. At its worst, the introduction of a cabinet system in, for example, a traditional Labour-dominated authority (which continued to organise itself in such a way that the group retained its customary authority), would have the effect of removing a wide range of opportunities for public debate and public representation that currently exist in a committee system. Responses to the White Paper exhortations about public involvement could easily be routed into 'safe' or symbolic channels. Effective public participation depends on public knowledge about key decisions, which are likely to affect public interests as much if not more than the opportunity to influence strategy or policy. Cabinet government (as at Westminster) will decrease rather than increase such decision-related opportunities unless the cabinet chooses to take remedial action.

Best Value and Public Participation

There is a tension also between 'enhanced public participation' and the Best Value proposals in the White Paper. Public participation is never 'cost free'. It adds to the cost of providing (or commissioning) a service. In situations where it involves the consultation of service user groups in an attempt to improve service quality and responsiveness, there is a potential justification under the 'effectiveness' heading. The service may cost more, but the cost may be worthwhile in terms of improved value to (or satisfaction of) the service user.

But for *deliberative* participation carried out in an attempt to gauge public feeling and allow public expression of views about a difficult choice facing a local authority – for example, a contentious planning proposal, town centre pedestrianisation scheme or a secondary schools rationalisation programme – it would in fact be difficult to demonstrate the *effectiveness* of a long period of consultation/participation. At best it could be argued that more people had been allowed to have their say or a wider range of views have been taken into account. The issue is perhaps best illustrated by the league table of local authority speed of response to planning applications. Quicker response rates may involve inadequate consultation in the interests of speed: slower response rates may involve better decisions in that the conflicting interests are better understood and weighed up. There are some difficult decisions here about identifying those issues where extended public participation is needed, separating them out from those where it is not.

Representative or Unrepresentative Participation?

Finally, a tension can be identified between the desire that public participation should be 'balanced' and 'representative' and the reality that it is often unbalanced and unrepresentative. Our case studies endorsed familiar conclusions from other research. There is often a low level of interest in public participation initiatives. Even within that low level, patterns of social exclusion are invariably reproduced. Young people and ethnic minority groups are particularly hard to reach. Such groups and others will often have had negative experiences with the council, and feel that members and officers do not take them seriously, which reinforces their predisposition that participation is unlikely to be worthwhile. One particularly effective route to the generation of apathy is the raising of expectations followed by an inability, or lack of preparedness to meet them. Meanwhile, more articulate and better-off social groups are well organised and well equipped to take advantage of public participation initiatives, particularly when their own interests are directly involved.

The implication is that in many areas there is a large amount of groundwork to be done before the desired level playing-field of participation can be delivered. A long experience of apathy, disappointment and low self-esteem has to be overcome. Most authorities we visited were well aware of the problem (though some took refuge in rather glib statements that public participation can reasonably be left to those who *want* to participate). But there is still a long way to go.

CONCLUSIONS

In the previous section, we set out a number of tensions which can be identified amongst the different proposal in the White Paper, and within the concept of participation itself. Local authorities will in effect have to make choices about the way in which they respond to the exhortations on public participation set out in the White Paper and in the Guidance Document which accompanies the DETR research report. There will be a temptation to marginalise the participation agenda *per se* in the light of the anticipated legislative requirements to introduce cabinet/mayoral systems of government. And more specifically there will be choices to be faced in relation to

- the extent to which information about cabinet decisions (or decision intentions) is (or is not) made publicly available in a way which facilitates participation;

- the extent to which the party group is prepared to allow its own preferences to be overruled by public preferences (and over what issues);

- the extent to which the council is prepared to extend its repertoire of participatory opportunities beyond 'traditional' and customer-oriented techniques' to include innovative consultative and deliberative methods, and ultimately a degree of empowerment;

- the extent to which authorities, are prepared to risk sub-optimal 'best value' performance measures in the interests of participation;

- the extent to which a council is prepared to make conscious efforts to encourage participation amongst groups who are currently disinclined to participate, and so increase the representativeness of local participation, or whether it merely provides participatory opportunities and argues that 'if people want to participate, they can'.

There will be authorities who have already developed a commitment to participation who are likely to react positively to the above set of choices, that is to open up information on cabinet decisions (and be prepared to overturn or delay them); to be flexible about the decision-making authority of the group (and, where relevant, local party); to develop innovative methods which move towards (in appropriate circumstances) power-sharing and devolution; to seek means of reaching traditional non-participants; and to be relaxed about the impact of a commitment to participation on 'Best Value' indications. But the crucial question is the extent to which the majority of authorities who are not necessarily philosophically disposed to enhanced participation will respond to these choices.

In relation to this issue there are important differences between the major parties. Public participation has long been a familiar element of the local political philosophy of the Liberal Democrats. Indeed, their enthusiasm for community politics (of which public consultation and participation are key elements) has been a key factor in their surge of electoral success since the early 1980s (Wilson and Game, 1998). The London boroughs of Richmond and Sutton have a long history of innovation in this respect since they became Liberal Democrat controlled in 1982 and 1986 respectively. Conservative Party groups have the least enthusiasm for the public participation agenda. One particular concern is the costs involved in consulting the public. Of the three major parties it is the Conservatives who support most strongly the 'representative democracy' model and often dismiss public participation as an abdication of political responsibility. As noted earlier, reactions in local Labour Party groups are more mixed, with traditional Labour holding a similar perspective to the Conservatives whereas 'New Labour' groups are usually more open-minded about participation, supporting initiatives such as citizens' juries and referenda.

As we have already implied, there is in our view a real danger that in many authorities the participatory agenda may become marginalised. It would not be difficult in the current legislative context for local authorities to concentrate their energies on customer-oriented methods, which, it can be argued, do little to improve *political* participation in local government. Indeed, it is possible to argue that they distract from political participation because they enable individuals to interact with public bodies as customers rather than citizens, thus avoiding the messy complexities of politics (Pratchett, 1998). Genuinely deliberative modes of participation, which engage with participants as citizens are not likely to be a requirement (on the basis of the White Paper text).

Our survey showed that superficially current council innovations in public participation respond well to government's democratic renewal agenda, with at best a healthy and positive attitude towards public participation being displayed. However, as a colleague has argued elsewhere (Pratchett, 1998):

> By examining these innovations in relation to more demanding democratic criteria it is apparent that most participation initiatives do little to enhance democratic responsiveness or increase political equality. Indeed, many of them seem to militate against these objectives. It is difficult to avoid the conclusion that most authorities are responding to the rhetoric of democratic renewal and enhanced public participation, rather than the democratic principles which supposedly underlie it. The consequence will be that while a select few authorities will achieve new levels of autonomy by 'pushing the right buttons' on the Government's democratic renewal check list, the more fundamental problems of democratic legitimacy and unresponsive political institutions which have beset local government for decades are unlikely to be resolved by the current experiments. Any attempt to build a case for greater local autonomy, which is based on such weak foundations, is surely destined to fail.

Public participation need not and arguably should not (as some councillors fear) replace the right of a democratically elected local council to make 'balanced' decisions, by a populist approach which responds to those who shout loudest. The challenge for a local authority is to develop criteria for deciding which issues are not appropriate for public participation and which are: in which case there is the secondary question of what methods should be used. There is also the choice, where public participation is justifiable, of when the final decision should remain with the council (but with an enhanced obligation to explain why it made the decision it did) and when decisions can appropriately be devolved to representative groups of service users or local residents. If such issues can be resolved, representative democracy and participatory democracy can operate as processes which add value to each other, rather than result in conflict.

NOTES

1. The research reported here is based upon research for the Department of the Environment, Transport and the Regions in 1998 undertaken by a joint De Montfort/Strathclyde University team consisting of Vivien Lowndes, Gerry Stoker, Lawrence Pratchett, David Wilson and the current authors.
2. Detailed case studies were carried out in 11 local authorities, involving interviews with officers and members and focus groups with members of the public who had been involved with a range of participation initiatives.
3. In relation to the Labour Party there is likely to be a parallel concern on the part of local Labour parties that public participation, if it moves beyond familiar consultation procedures, may challenge the right of local parties to formulate policy

REFERENCES

Arnstein, S., 1971, 'A Ladder of Citizen Participation', *Journal of the Royal Town Planning Institute*, Vol.57, No.4, pp.176–82.

Copus, C., 1998, 'The Party Group: Model Standing Orders and a Discipline Approach to Representation', *Local Government Studies*, Vol.25, No.3.

DETR, 1998, *Modern Local Government: In Touch with the People*, Cm.4014 (London: HMSO).

DETR, 1999, *Local Leadership, Local Choice*, Cm.4298 (London: HMSO).

Game, C. and S. Leach, 1995, *The Role of Political Parties in Local Democracy* (CLD Report No.11, London, Commission for Local Democracy/Municipal Journal Books).

Lowndes, V. *et al.*, 1998a, *Enhancing Public Participation in Local Government: A Research Report* (London: DETR).

Lowndes, V. *et al.*, 1998b, *Guidance on Enhancing Public Participation in Local Government* (London: DETR).

Pratchett, L., 1998, 'Public Participation and the Case for More Local Autonomy in the UK' (Conference Paper: University of Humboldt, Berlin, 10–12 Dec. 1998).

Stewart, J., 1995, *Innovation in Democratic Practice* (Birmingham: School of Public Policy, Birmingham University).

Young, K. and M. Davies, 1990, *The Politics of Local Government since Widdicombe* (York: Joseph Rowntree Foundation).

Researching Public Participation

MARIAN BARNES

In an article entitled 'Research and User Involvement: Contributions to Learning and Methods', Gerald Wistow and I argued that research had an important role to play both as means of enabling users' voices to be heard, and as a means of understanding more about 'user involvement' itself – what it means for the users who become involved, for the agencies seeking to hear from those who use their services, and how the benefits to both might be maximised (Barnes and Wistow, 1992). At the time we were engaged in what was then a rather innovative project involving collaboration between a local authority and health authorities in order to involve people who use services in developing both the policy and practice of community care (Barnes and Wistow, 1994). The Department of Health had considered the Birmingham Community Care Special Action Project (CCSAP) suitably significant to warrant funding an evaluation in order to learn the lessons of this way of working and to contribute to supporting similar developments elsewhere.

As others in this collection have demonstrated, 'user involvement' is no longer a radical new idea. Nor is the commitment to go beyond the direct users of particular services to engage with citizens generally both in developing policy and in designing services. Developments are not only taking place in local government, but throughout the public sector. In the health service, for example, following the exhortation to health authorities to become 'Champions of the People' (NHSME, 1992) methods of engaging with communities to determine health needs, to consult over service commissioning and in determining priorities have developed alongside initiatives to hear directly from those using health services (see, for example, Barnes, 1997; Lupton *et al.*, 1998). This is not just a matter of seeking to produce more responsive public services, but of developing more dialogic mechanisms of public accountability. This latter purpose is becoming more central as public bodies with very different accountability structures are encouraged not only to work in partnership with each other, but with the communities and citizens they serve. In the context of health action zones, new deal for communities, crime and disorder strategies and

Marian Barnes, University of Birmingham

other policy arenas, communities and citizens have been identified as deliverers of public policies and as participants in the new governance mechanisms which are emerging to secure co-ordinated action on cross-cutting policy issues.

As user involvement and citizen participation have become part of mainstream policy and, indeed, both required tasks for public service officials and a means of delivering public policy, the wish to know 'what works best' and 'how to do it' has become ever stronger. The current policy environment is characterised by calls for evidence-based practice from a government shy of ideology and searching out examples of good practice on which to base policy. In this context evidence of what works generated by independent evaluation is increasingly being called for. One example of this is the Department of Health's policy research programme, 'Health in Partnership', launched in 1998. This places a strong emphasis on the evaluation of different methods of both individual and collective involvement in health care and health policy decision making.

This article considers the design of evaluations of public participation and the criteria which might be used to assess the success of such initiatives. The analysis is based on the author's own experience of researching user and citizen participation in different contexts and on other research in this area. It also considers how far *evaluation* may be able to answer critical questions which are emerging as public participation moves into the mainstream and at what point it might be more appropriate to talk about 'researching' rather than 'evaluating' public participation.

PUBLIC POLICY MAKING AND PUBLIC PARTICIPATION

Objectives and forms of public participation are wide-ranging and varied. The development of more participatory approaches to citizen involvement is being pursued in the context of specific services or policies, and in the context of action within local areas to enable people to take part in both defining and responding to key issues within localities. Action with communities is seen as a route to community regeneration, community safety, and to improvements in the health of populations. Citizen participation is considered to be a necessary condition for a cohesive society and a route to reducing social exclusion. Public authorities are seeking to legitimate their actions by more direct involvement with their publics and to establish more direct and dynamic accountability mechanisms. More participatory approaches to service delivery are being developed to achieve both greater responsiveness and better outcomes.

Whilst commitment to user and citizen participation is growing, new methods of working with citizens represent a challenge to many of those whose professional training has taught them to separate themselves from those to whom they provide services. They can also be threatening to elected members who regard themselves as *the* legitimate representatives of the people. Public involvement can be seen as complicating the already difficult process of reaching decisions about complex and disputed policy issues. Involving the public in decision making can be expensive, time-consuming and frustrating because it may prevent planned change taking place. Officials sometimes complain that the public is apathetic because it fails to respond to opportunities to have its say.

Opening up opportunities for public participation does not necessarily lead to consensus, nor are such opportunities always seen to be consistent with the objectives of self-organised user and community groups. Deliberation is taking place not only between citizens and officials, but also amongst excluded groups and groups whose members share identities which are being articulated through the process of collective action (see, for example, Campbell and Oliver, 1996; Williams and Schoultz, 1984). Community and user groups provide opportunities for participation within safe environments and can support people in taking part in dialogues with officials. But such groups may also reject invitations to take part in policy making in circumstances in which they have not been involved in defining the agenda and determining the rules of engagement.

Evaluation in this context needs to reflect the reality of a complex and contested set of perspectives and purposes. Evaluation questions need to incorporate the pragmatic concerns of those who want to improve the practice of citizen participation, as well as a broader and more theoretical purpose in understanding what such developments mean for the relationship between state and citizens. In order to answer questions about how successful different methods of enabling citizen participation might be in achieving wide-ranging objectives relating to increasing and improving the nature and level of citizen involvement in decision making about public services, and in contributing to the broader democratic project implied by such action, it is important to distinguish the nature and purpose of different models of participation.

A FRAMEWORK FOR THE ANALYSIS OF CITIZEN PARTICIPATION

The following analysis is based on a framework developed with colleagues in the School of Public Policy at the University of Birmingham (Barnes *et al.*, 1997). Models of citizen participation vary on a number of dimensions:

1. *Whose participation is being sought?* A distinction between user and citizen participation has already been suggested, although it is also

important to recognise that 'consumers' are also 'citizens' and thus may have both particular and broader interests in public services and decision-making processes. But apart from this distinction, the focus may be on people who share identities relating to gender, age, ethnic or cultural group, or who live in particular places or circumstances which may result in shared experiences. Some methods of participation seek to involve a cross-section or 'representative' group of citizens living in a particular area. Others seek to prioritise people who may often be excluded from decision making.

2. *The type of knowledge to be accessed through the process of participation.* Knowledge may be categorised as 'expert', 'interested', 'informed' or 'un-informed'. Thus the objective may be to enable the participation of people who already have reason to be knowledgeable about the subject under consideration because of personal experience (experiential knowledge); to increase the knowledge of citizens generally through the process of participation and thus to access informed public opinion; or to explore uninformed views of those who have no particular reason for specialist interest or knowledge and who have not gained knowledge through the process of having their say.

3. *The location within which participation is being sought.* Those initiating action to engage with the public occupy different positions within the public sphere, and, increasingly within non-public bodies. They may be elected members seeking to develop their contacts with constituents through the creation of local area sub-committees. Action from within service systems may be taken by service commissioners, or by providers. Research and policy organisations, such as the Institute for Public Policy Research, and consortia of public and private bodies, such as the Millennium Debate of the Age, have also taken the initiative to explore the views of citizens about public policy issues. The impetus for action can also come from amongst community groups, user groups or voluntary groups, that is from organised groups of citizens seeking access to decision-making processes.

4. *The objectives and purposes of participation.* Citizens who are also users of services may be seeking to change the nature of the services they receive, but they may also be seeking broader social change objectives. Objectives may be to enable citizens to become empowered to take more control over their lives, to build social capital and reduce social exclusion, to enable service providers to learn more about how people experience using their service, or to increase the accountability of officials to their publics. Participation may be seen as an end as well as a means to other ends.

5. *The degree of power sharing implied through opening up opportunities for public participation.* In some cases this can involve delegation or sharing of decision-taking powers, for example in relating to the use of budgets or appointments of new staff. In some cases the agenda is set by citizens or by citizens in negotiation with officials. But often people are invited to participate in deliberation in relation to issues which have been defined by officials, but not to define the issues, or take part in decision *taking.*

6. *The scope of participation and the level at which change may be achieved.* This could be:

- in individual decision making
- at group, community or neighbourhood level
- at the level of particular social, health or environmental programmes
- in relation to particular organisations
- at the level of policy making.

Methods of participation can be distinguished by reference to each of the above dimensions, but the dimensions are also interrelated. Thus, the issue of whose participation is sought is closely related to the type of knowledge being accessed. A more useful approach to distinguishing key dimensions of different models of participation may be to map these along intersecting axes. For example, models of participation may be distinguished by reference to their focus on consumer or citizens, and whether they approach people as individuals or collectively (see Figure 1).

This framework is a heuristic device to distinguish different 'types' of participation initiatives for the purpose of evaluation. It is not intended as a classificatory system to 'fix' any particular action in one location. Because

FIGURE 1

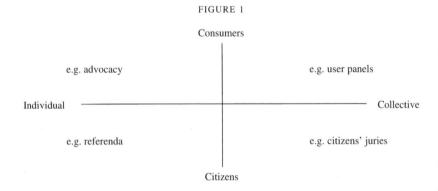

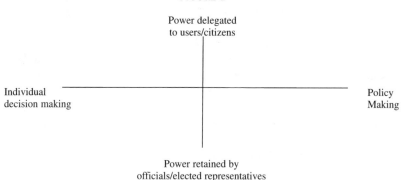

FIGURE 2

Power delegated
to users/citizens

Individual
decision making

Policy
Making

Power retained by
officials/elected representatives

of this it would also be possible to use other dimensions of participation to define axes which would highlight other aspects of participation. Another might relate to the level at which participation is sought and the degree of power delegated, as in Figure 2.

One practical implication of this analysis is that any agency wanting to develop a comprehensive strategy for public participation needs to apply different models for different ends (for example, IHSM, NHS Confederation, NHSE, 1998). A key implication for evaluation is that the questions to be addressed are strategic rather than straightforwardly comparative. That is they are concerned with the contribution different methods or models of participation can play within an overall strategy, rather than which single method is best. This article discusses opportunities for collective participation rather than models, such as advocacy, which support greater individual involvement in decision making.

EVALUATING CITIZEN PARTICIPATION

Positivist models of evaluation require programme or policy objectives to be set and criteria defined and measured in order to determine the degree of success. They assume that goals are, or can be, clearly stated, that there is only one view as to what those goals are, and that objective measurement of goal achievement is possible. The appropriateness of this model has been convincingly critiqued by many engaged in public policy analysis and in the study of service delivery processes.

Alternative evaluation models have been developed in the context of public policy which aim to reflect the contested and dynamic nature of the process of policy making, the diffuse and hard to measure objectives which are often implicit rather than explicit, and a process of implementation which often results in a recasting or development of objectives as a result of experience (for example, Barnes, 1993; Finne *et al.*, 1995). Such models emphasise the importance of evaluation as a process of learning rather than judging (Rebien, 1996; Stewart and Walsh, 1994). Evaluation questions are couched in terms of 'what are the conditions for success?' and 'why/how has this initiative been successful (or not)?' rather than solely by reference to the measurement of previously specified objectives. In some cases the process of evaluation may itself be the means through which participants clarify what they mean by the action in which they are engaged. This was the case, for example, in an evaluation of community relations carried out in Northern Ireland (Knox, 1995). Not only were there no reliable quantifiable indicators of what 'success' might mean in terms of community relations activities, there was no broadly based understanding and agreement about what the term 'community relations' actually means. The design of evaluation in such circumstances is intended to enable learning amongst those actively engaged in the programme which is the subject of evaluation. Such evaluation has many of the characteristics of action research, contributing to the process of development as well as learning about the activity which is the subject of the research.

Evaluation of public participation has to recognise the political nature of the participative process and reflect in the way the evaluation itself is conducted the importance of enabling different voices to be heard. As we have seen, the purposes of public participation are not just concerned with the achievement of service or policy outcomes, but also relate to social exclusion and social cohesion and the achievement of democratic renewal. Evaluators are citizens as well as researchers and evaluation can contribute to or frustrate the cause of democracy and social justice to which citizen participation is intended to contribute (Greene, 1996; House, 1993).

Pluralistic evaluation involves the identification of different stakeholders and seeks to establish how well the service or programme performs according to criteria defined by different stakeholders (Smith and Cantley, 1988). Empowerment evaluation (Fetterman *et al.*, 1996) takes the stakeholder analysis a stage further to identify power relationships amongst stakeholders. It aims to contribute to social change by prioritising the perspectives of those who have been disadvantaged or excluded from power. When the subject of evaluation is itself a process intended to enable marginalised or excluded groups to play a part in decision making (as, for example, in the case of community development), then engaging participants in evaluating both the process and outcomes of such activity is integral to the achievement of overall objectives.

These principles have been applied in different ways in evaluations of participation projects. For example, the evaluation of CCSAP used a number of methods to engage people as direct participants in the evaluation process. The most intensive of these involved two groups of carers who met regularly in order to define evaluation criteria, to design data collection instruments and respond to evidence of action being taken by the city as part of the action programme. Carer involvement in the evaluation of CCSAP was an important part of a continuing process of developing opportunities for carers to be involved in service development. The carers' panels, established for the evaluation, continued to meet after the research had been completed as a forum for continuing input into decision making.

EVALUATING PROCESSES AND OUTCOMES

In situations in which policy or service outcomes are uncertain and may take some time to realise, the intrinsic benefits of participation are important to make it worth people's while to take part. Many public participation initiatives seek change in the participants themselves. They seek to create more informed citizens who are more able to deliberate issues of public policy, they aim to enable people to become more confident in speaking up on their own and others' behalves, and they seek to re-build the trust and confidence that citizens and users have in public services and those who provide them. A key objective is the creation of a healthier, more active democracy. This means that the process of participation should itself be the subject of analysis to assess whether or not it meets criteria of democratic participation and enables participants to experience direct benefit from taking part.

Gastil has considered the process of democracy as it operates within small groups:

> A small group is democratic if it has equally distributed decision-making power, an inclusive membership committed to democracy, healthy relationships among its members, and a democratic method of deliberation. Group deliberation is democratic if group members have equal and adequate opportunities to speak, neither withhold information nor verbally manipulate one another, and are able and willing to listen. (Gastil, 1993: 6)

The notion of 'deliberation' is central to collective models of public participation. Deliberation can take place amongst groups of citizens and between citizens and officials. It can take place in citizens' juries, consensus conferences, user panels and joint planning meetings. Many groups who have experienced powerlessness and exclusion find benefit in separate opportunities for articulating and developing their particular experiences before entering fora in which they deliberate with people in positions of power. Gutman and Thompson identify three principles underpinning deliberative democracy: reciprocity, publicity and accountability, and describe the overall purpose as to 'promote extensive moral argument about the merits of public policies in public forums, with the aim of reaching provisional moral agreement and maintaining mutual respect among citizens' (1996: 12). A commitment to deliberation is based on a recognition that there are different value positions affecting public policy making which need to be resolved through dialogue rather than by the exercise of power. Evaluation of collective processes of public participation must explore directly the process of deliberation.

If public participation is to be a route to improved social cohesion and social justice it is important to question the extent to which opportunities for public participation offer the possibility for people to take part who rarely do so. In this context, the criteria for evaluating forums in which deliberation takes place need to include the following:

1. *Is the process of deliberation equally accessible to all those intended to be able to take part?* Personal motivation is rarely the sole reason for people not taking part. Women and older people may fear leaving the house alone. Frail older people may be unable to travel without assistance. People who because of poverty or social exclusion have had no experience of being able to exercise control over their own lives may see little value in taking part in deliberative fora where the rules have been set and the agenda determined by powerful officials.

Some forms of public participation are intended to provide an opportunity for any citizen to take part. In very different ways both open public meetings and citizens' juries are intended to provide opportunities for citizens in a wide range of circumstances to become involved, although public meetings depend on people deciding to take part and citizens' juries invite a sample of citizens. In contrast, stakeholder conferences are intended to provide an opportunity for users of specific services to deliberate with provider and other stakeholders, user panels bring together people sharing experiences of using particular services, whilst community groups define their target membership by reference to a particular community identity. The application of this criterion will vary depending on the nature of the initiative, but the principle is the same – is the model of participation capable of including any amongst the target group, or are there aspects of the model *per se* which would systematically exclude people in particular circumstances? For example, groups based around identities as disabled people or users of mental health services have acknowledged their difficulties in involving black people. Identity-based groups depend on people accepting those identities as a basis for collective action. In contrast, citizen's juries aim to include a cross-section of citizens. But a recent evaluation indicated no disabled people were involved and no people over 70 took part. The practical organisation of citizen's juries affect their capacity to include disabled people, whilst the intensive nature of the process may systematically exclude frail older people (Barnes, 1999).

2. *Is the process of deliberation an inclusive one?* The issue of inclusivity goes beyond the question of whether or not anyone in the target group can access the forum in which deliberation is taking place. Webler has developed what he calls an 'evaluative yardstick' for the purpose of assessing whether models of citizen participation meet criteria of competence and fairness in deliberation. The normative nature of the criteria proposed by Webler to evaluate deliberation – competence and fairness – could be construed as requiring communication skills which are unequally shared between different groups within the population. He recognises the potential difficulty:

> Except for the most obvious cases of mental illness and the inability to use language (and even here it is sometimes difficult to draw a clear line), excluding participation opportunities based on assessments of individuals' cognitive competence is unethical. Even lingual incompetence in the dominant language is not an excuse to legitimately exclude a citizen – translators should be hired. (Webler, 1995)

Those active in mental health user groups would not only agree that it is unethical to exclude people on the basis of diagnosed mental illness, but, through their engagement with strategic issues of mental health service planning and their involvement in the education and training of mental health workers, would point to the misguided association between mental illness and incompetence to engage in deliberation on issues of public policy. The issue is whether the way in which deliberation is conducted privileges groups who communicate in a particular way and who are privy to particular types of knowledge. Inclusivity is not just an issue of access to the forum, but of access to the deliberative process within it. The importance of enabling dialogue between people who occupy different social positions and who bring to the process perspectives deriving from the experiential knowledge of those circumstances is reflected in Young's analysis of the significance of deliberation as a means of challenging dominant assumptions about norms and values:

> group representation unravels the false consensus that cultural imperialism may have produced, and reveals group bias in norms,

standards, styles and perspectives that have been assumed as universal or of highest value. By giving voice to formerly silenced or devalued needs and experiences, groups representation forces participants in discussion to take a reflective distance on their assumptions and think beyond their own interests. When confronted with interests, needs and opinions that derived from very different social positions and experience, persons sometimes come to understand the limitations of their own experience and perspective for coming to conclusions about the best policy for everyone. (Young, quoted in Phillips, 1993)

But before such reflective distance is possible the language used in discussion must be accessible to non-experts as well as experts, the process needs to be capable of embracing different styles of communication and emotional expressions of anger and frustration which come from exclusion. Evidence from early experiences of involving users of mental health services in discussions about psychiatric services demonstrated that professionals trained to conduct debate in a 'rational' manner can find the 'raw anger' of those who have had no voice in decision making very threatening. This can lead them to deny the legitimacy of experiences expressed in language which does not conform to a 'professional' norm (Barnes and Wistow, 1994).

3. *Do different forms of deliberation and participation have the capacity to engage not only with difference but also dissent?* The greater the potential for inclusiveness the greater the diversity of experience which will be represented within deliberative forums. An absence of dissent is not necessarily a positive indicator. Nor is obtaining a consensus output necessarily the only desirable outcome of deliberative processes which are not established to act as decision arbiters. The capacity of deliberative methods to enable difference and dissent to be identified, engaged with and understood may be a more important indicator of their 'success' than whether or not a consensus decision is reached at the end. This was the view of participants in a citizens' jury invited to reflect on evaluation criteria. They did not see a necessity to reach agreement, but they did consider that the way in which differences of view were handled within the process was a significant indicator of success. This particular jury was conducted in Belfast and this may have affected the awareness of participants of the importance of engaging positively with different views (Barnes, 1999).

4. *Does the process enable 'experts' to be challenged?* If dominant assumptions are to be challenged through a process of enabling citizens to take part in policy making, then the process must allow for the 'experts' and their 'expertise' to be challenged. This is a vital part of the process of ensuring greater public accountability and is necessary in any attempt to

shift the balance between expert and citizen decision making. If public participation is understood solely as 'educating' or 'informing' the public then the potential for officials to learn from the public is lost. One example of this comes from an evaluation of user panels involving frail older people. Local social work and health officials were invited to meet with panels of older people to discuss issues of concern identified by panel members. Some officials saw this as a process of explaining to the panel members why their concerns could not be answered. Others were much more open to learning from the older people about the shortcomings of existing procedures or services. But the fact that officials were being invited in to meet the older people on their territory, to respond to issues collectively identified and discussed prior to their arrival, meant that it was easier to put officials in the position of having to answer questions than is the case when users are invited to join official decision making fora and are in a clear minority in such settings (Barnes and Bennet, 1998).

5. *Does it make a difference to participants?* The key purpose of deliberation is to achieve change. Change will only come about if people develop new ideas, new ways of looking at the world, new understandings. Thus a criterion for evaluating deliberative methods is whether or not the process enables the participants to learn through taking part. As I have suggested above, the learning process must be a two-way one. Officials need to be open to learning from citizens and the process must be one which enables the citizens who take part to learn and develop themselves.

Public participation is both a means and an end. The process itself, if it meets the criteria suggested above, can be a means of achieving change in those who are part of it. The service and policy outcomes of participation are uncertain for public service officials as well as for citizens, not least because of the multiplicity of factors which will influence those outcomes. This implies that participation must provide intrinsic benefits if people are to be motivated to take part. Participation must provide value *per se* to participants – both citizens and officials. For citizens that value will often consist of increased knowledge, understanding or information; of enhanced capacities to engage in deliberation; an enhanced sense of self-esteem and self-worth deriving from the knowledge that their views and knowledge are valued; as well as benefits deriving from the social contact, friendship and support offered by collective organisation or action. For officials, organisational learning and improved public confidence and legitimacy are likely to be important. Some have also talked of the enjoyment that comes from engaging directly with local people and the renewed sense of commitment to their work. These intrinsic benefits can also be considered outcomes or impacts of participation.

6. *Does it make a difference more broadly?* All those who take part hope that their involvement will make a difference beyond the forum itself. The underlying rationale for increasing public participation is that this will provide outcomes in policies, practices, organisations and systems that are of public benefit. If participation is a route out of social exclusion, not only should the process be inclusive, but so too should the outcomes. Whilst direct cause and effect may be difficult to pin down, and the time-scales in which change might become evident fall outside the funding periods of evaluative research, changes in the type of policy decisions reached and in perceptions of the health of the democratic process are longer term indicators of the collective impact of citizen deliberation. There is an assumption that including people previously excluded from decision-making processes will make a difference to the policy outcomes. We need to know whether this is indeed the case, and if not, why not.

In her evaluation of citizens' juries commissioned by health authorities, McIver (1997) considered the immediate response of the health authorities to the jury recommendations. She found that jury recommendations had influenced decision making, although mainly by 'adding weight' to issues and thus giving them higher priority, rather than by suggesting radical alternatives. Do officials only take action on those recommendations with which they agree?

User groups face dilemmas about the extent to which they should take part in official fora and add credibility to decisions dominated by professional and political concerns. Mental health user members of a national task force set up to develop service standards resigned from this when it became clear that users' views were being over-ridden in relation to fundamental issues affecting a review of the Mental Health Act. Political considerations fuelled by media profiling of a small number of incidents involving murders committed by discharged psychiatric patients outweighed widespread user (and professional) views about the nature of changes required. Such experiences cause users to question the value of engaging in dialogue when outcomes are determined by factors outside the process itself.

CONDUCTING EVALUATIONS OF PARTICIPATION

The design of evaluations of public participation is only partly about defining questions and criteria. Methods of conducting evaluations also need to reflect the nature of the processes which are the subject of study. In spite of the increasing theoretical and methodological sophistication being developed by evaluators who adopt naturalistic rather than experimental methods, the hegemony of positivistic models of research remains strong.

The evaluator faces conflicting dilemmas in this situation. On the one hand, those engaged in innovative participation projects may be reluctant to agree to be evaluated because this is seen as inappropriate scrutiny of practices intended to achieve objectives which cannot be measured. On the other hand, models of evaluation based on more reflexive approaches to research which are designed to explore the experiences and perceptions of the participants may not achieve credibility amongst key decision makers.

Researchers evaluating public participation need to learn to work in different ways from those which have traditionally been considered to comprise the repertoire of research skills. They need to become facilitators, consultants and co-workers, rather than external experts brought in to pass judgement on performance. But at the same time they need to demonstrate that these approaches to evaluation are rigorous and capable of being subject to scrutiny. The key issues in the conduct of evaluation in this context can be summarised as follows:

- Evaluation needs to recognise the different perspectives of different stakeholders in the process and to consider how the different positions of power occupied by stakeholders may affect not only their perspectives on the process of participation, but the weight to be given to those perspectives in drawing conclusions about participating.

- The evaluation process itself should adopt participatory methods consistent with the principles of participation and enable participants to be part of the learning process.

- Data collection methods need to reflect the pluralistic and participatory design indicated above. Multiple data collection methods are likely to be necessary, and the process of analysis is likely to be interactive and iterative.

- The overall purpose of evaluation should emphasise learning rather than judgement. Results should be publicly available and accessible for debate.

IN CONCLUSION: EVALUATION OR RESEARCH?

Interest in the practical development of new ways of involving citizens has been accompanied by a wish on the part of those investing in such processes to know if they worked and if they made a difference. This is usually constructed as a need to undertake evaluations of different methods of enabling public participation. However, questions about the effectiveness of different methods need to reflect the nature and purpose of different approaches. It is not so much an issue of 'what works best?' as 'what contribution can different approaches make to an overall strategy for enabling public participation?' In addition, the evaluation criteria discussed in this article do not lend themselves to straightforward tick box analysis. They require an analysis of the meanings different participants attach to the same process, of the power relations between the players involved, of the way in which particular forms of communicating or particular experiences may affect the perceived legitimacy of the contributions offered by participants to the deliberative process. They also require an understanding of the backgrounds and circumstances of the different 'publics' such initiatives aim to involve and how this might affect not only what they bring to the process, but also whether or not the process is one which has any perceived relevance to their lives. And in terms of the impact of public participation on policy and service development, there is a need to understand the policy context and the range of factors within that which might affect both the preparedness and capacity of officials to respond to issues raised by the participative process. More broadly, this raises questions about the place of any particular initiative to involve the public within public policy decision making, and the contribution of such new methods to developing a more deliberative and participatory democracy. For example, is the relationship between a citizens' jury commissioned by a local authority and the elected members of that authority a different one from the relationship between a citizens' jury and non-elected health authority members?

The exploration of these type of issues may be better understood as a process of 'researching' rather than 'evaluating'. Whilst there is increasing recognition that evaluation needs to move out of the straight-jacket of measuring outcomes against a uni-dimensional set of predetermined objectives, there is also a need to convince policy makers that the evidence base on which decisions about complex and contested issues of public policy should be reached does not derive solely from the conduct of evaluations, but needs to include the broader understandings that research can bring.

REFERENCES

Barnes, M., 1993, 'Introducing New Stakeholders – User and Researcher Interests in Evaluative Research: A Discussion of Methods used to Evaluate the Birmingham Community Care Special Action Project', *Policy and Politics*, Vol.21, No.1, pp.47–58.
Barnes, M., 1997, *The People's Health Service?* (Birmingham: NHS Confederation).
Barnes, M., 1999, *Building a Deliberative Democracy. An Evaluation of Two Citizens' Juries* (London: Institute for Public Policy Research).
Barnes, M. and G. Bennet, 1998, 'Frail Bodies, Courageous Voices: Older People Influencing Community Care', *Health and Social Care in the Community*, Vol.6, No.2, pp.102–11.

Barnes, M. *et al.*, 1997, *Citizen Participation: A Framework for Evaluation* (School of Public Policy, University of Birmingham).

Barnes, M. and G. Wistow (eds.), 1992, *Researching User Involvement* (University of Leeds, Nuffield Institute for Health).

Barnes, M. and G. Wistow, 1994, 'Achieving a Strategy for User Involvement in Community Care', *Health and Social Care in the Community*, 2, pp.347–56.

Barnes, M. and G. Wistow, 1994, 'Learning to Hear Voices: Listening to Users of Mental Health Services', *Journal of Mental Health*, 3, pp.525–40.

Campbell, J. and M. Oliver, 1996, *Disability Politics* (London: Routledge).

Fetterman, D.M., S.J. Kaftarian and A. Wandersman (eds.), 1996, *Empowerment Evaluation: Knowledge and Tools for Self-Assessment and Accountability* (Thousand Oaks, CA: Sage).

Finne, H., M. Levin and T. Nilssen, 1995, 'Trailing Research: A Model for Useful Programme Evaluation', *Evaluation*, Vol.1, No.1, pp.11–31.

Gastil, J., 1993, *Democracy in Small Groups: Participation, Decision Making and Communication* (Philadelphia, PA: New Society Publishers).

Greene, J.C., 1996, 'Qualitative Evaluation and Scientific Citizenship: Reflections and Refractions', *Evaluation*, Vol.2, No.3, pp.277–89.

Gutmann, A. and D. Thompson, 1996, *Democracy and Disagreement* (Cambridge, MA: Harvard University Press).

House, E., 1993, *Professional Evaluation* (London and Newbury Park: Sage).

IHSM, NHS Confederation, NHSE, 1998, *In the Public Interest: Developing a Strategy for Public Participation in the NHS* (Leeds: NHSE).

Knox, C., 1995, 'Concept Mapping in Policy Evaluation: A Research Review of Community Relations in Northern Ireland', *Evaluation*, Vol.1, No.1, pp.65–80.

Lupton, C., S. Peckham and P. Taylor, 1998, *Managing Public Involvement in Healthcare Purchasing* (Buckingham: Open University Press).

McIver, S., 1997, *An Evaluation of the Kings Fund Citizens' Jury Programme* (University of Birmingham, Health Services Management Centre).

NHSME, 1992, *Local Voices. The Views of Local People in Purchasing for Health* (London: Department of Health).

Phillips, A., 1993, *Democracy and Difference* (Cambridge: Polity Press).

Rebien, C.C., 1996, 'Participatory Evaluation of Development Assistance: Dealing with Power and Facilitative Learning', *Evaluation*, Vol.2, No.2, pp.151–71.

Smith, G. and G. Cantley, 1988, 'Pluralistic Evaluation', in *Evaluation* Research Highlights on Social Work, 8 (London: Jessica Kinglsey).

Stewart, J. and K. Walsh, 1994, 'Performance Measurement: When Performance can never be Finally Defined', *Public Money and Management*, Vol.14, No.2, pp.49–50.

Webler, T., 1995, '"Right" Discourse in Citizen Participation', in O. Renn, T. Webler and P. Widemann (eds.), *Fairness and Competence in Citizen Participation. Evaluating Models for Environmental Discourse* (Dordrecht: Kluwer Academic Publishers).

Williams, P. and B. Schoultz, 1984, *We can Speak for Ourselves* (Bloomington, IN: Indiana University Press).

The Party Group:
A Barrier to Democratic Renewal

COLIN COPUS

Local government political management structures are a product of the Victorian era; the committee system, originating from that time, was once seen as a strength of local democracy, reflecting important political conflicts. The battles between improvers and economisers, radicals and conservatives, and between local autonomy and national control, were played out in the council committees of the nineteenth century. Meanwhile, councillors were developing their own private decision-making forum – the party group – and experiencing varying levels of success, across time and place, in ensuring that councillors acted as coherent bodies around some policy or label (Owen, 1968; Young, 1972; Hennock, 1973; Young, 1975; Young and Garside, 1982; Newton, 1982; Saint, 1989).

The democratic renewal project reflects the view that the political structures of local government fail to result in transparent, responsive and accountable decision making. The committee system is seen as laborious, disguising and dissipating responsibility and immersing councillors in too much administrative detail, distancing them from wider representative concerns. In addition, committee, and indeed the council, has for some time ceased to be the place where decisions are made, but is where the majority group ratifies the outcomes of its private meetings. Thus, the group has become the most important theatre for local representation (Hampton, 1970; Jones, 1975; Saunders, 1979; Stoker, 1991; Game and Leach, 1995). Whilst internally democratic bodies groups are inherently anti-democratic, in that councillor loyalty places the group between, and above, the electorate and councillor. The group represents a set of entrenched political interests benefiting from the processes of local representative democracy, and has the potential to thwart, distort or shape the outcomes of the democratic renewal project.

The modernisation agenda for local government set out in 'Local Democracy and Community Leadership' (HMSO, 1998), the White Paper, 'Modern Local Government: In Touch with the People' and the draft bill

Colin Copus, University of Wolverhampton Business School

'Local Leadership: Local Choice' (HMSO, 1999) represents a major challenge to the way councillors organise themselves into groups and do business. The intention that local political decision making will become more open, transparent and accountable challenges the private nature of much of that decision making which takes place in group meetings. Indeed, the White Paper and draft bill recognises that the party group can damage accountability and transparency (para. 3.4) – a recognition reflected by the national Labour Party (Labour Party, 1999). Yet the renewal project has so far failed to account adequately for the party group as the antithesis of open, transparent and responsive local government and to develop a strategy to transform the group system into an open and accountable political process. The party group is not linked to the wider diagnosis of local democracy – a serious omission.

A further challenge for the group system arises from the proposed separation of councillors' executive and scrutiny roles and the introduction of executive leaders and cabinets or directly elected mayors. These new political management structures will require councillors to publicly scrutinise members of an executive, which could comprise their own party colleagues. Indeed, the draft bill goes so far as to set out a duty on councillors to publicly question and criticise the executive 'even if from the same political party' (para.3.13). Yet it fails to address the cultural leap required in British local government to generate the political environment where councillors can regularly and willingly criticise their group in public. It contains no analysis of the group as a closed and private theatre in which local political decisions are made – decisions to which councillors are publicly bound, and thus often brought into conflict with articulated community opinion.

The party group, that coherent and disciplined body of councillors acting under the same party label – whose independent existence was demonstrated by Gyford and James (1983) – has a profound influence over the processes of local democracy. An influence that conflicts with the democratic renewal project to re-engage local government with communities and open up decision making to public scrutiny. This paper examines the barrier to the democratic renewal project represented by the party group system. The first section defines local democracy in terms of its openness and transparency, questioning whether the representative nature of local government is sufficient to ensure citizen participation in political processes. It goes on to consider how the group and committee systems work to obfuscate local democracy. The second section explores the group as the most important theatre for conducting council business. The third examines councillors' attitudes towards the electorate. The final section draws on the material presented to set out the consequences for the democratic renewal project of the influence of the party group; it considers how the group and leader and cabinet model – as the most likely to be adopted – may interact. The data presented in this paper was drawn from a research project into the party group system, which involved a questionnaire survey of over 600 councillors, in-depth interviews, case studies and participant observation.

LOCAL DEMOCRACY AND THE PARTY GROUP

Political representation involves a transfer of engagement from the citizen to the elected representative, facilitated through the mechanism of the political party. Liberal democracy, based as it is on two propositions – the electoral assumption and competitive elitism – enables the citizen to select between local political elites (Held, 1993). Indeed, some hold that this selection is all that is required of the citizen to participate in the political processes (Sartori, 1962; Schumpeter, 1974). Moreover, much democratic theorising has been less about securing responsive and transparent government and more about reconciling support for a system of popular democracy with protecting minority privilege against majoritarian threats to property rights (Beloff, 1948; Crick, 1982; Held, 1993; de Tocqueville, 1994). Indeed, the local government franchise as it developed throughout the nineteenth century ensured that those exercising the vote, and the candidates from which they could select, fulfilled some property qualification (Keith-Lucas, 1952; Hennock, 1973). British local government developed not as representative democracy but a 'form of ratepayer democracy' (Young, 1989; also Gyford, 1986; Davis, 1989; Gillespie, 1989).

That local government is elected is alone insufficient to label it democratic, as representative democracy is designed as an alternative to self-rule and on-going wide-scale citizen participation in the processes of political decision making (Manin, 1997). The value of local government to democracy lies not so much in that it is a representative body, legitimised by the public vote, but rather in a wider interpretation of democracy (Cochrane, 1986). The democratic renewal agenda provides clues to how local democracy can be defined by the opportunities it provides for citizen participation in local political decision making (Almond and Verba, 1963; Marsh, 1977; Kavanagh, 1989; Parry et al., 1992) – as J.S. Mill saw it, a developmental participation encouraging citizens to see beyond their specific interests – its responsiveness to citizen concerns, and the degree of openness and transparency of its political processes.

A definition of local democracy based on wide-ranging participation by the citizenry rests on the responsiveness of councillors to articulated community demands (Bulpitt, 1972; Parry, 1977; 1992). The party group system, however, serves to delocalise local issues and to widen the councillor's scope of representation away from local communities to a broader concern with governing the area (Glassberg, 1981; Muchnick, 1970; Lambert et al., 1978; Copus, 1997; 1998). Participation and responsiveness also rest on the openness of the political processes so that those participating are able to observe councillors deliberating and responding to complex local political issues, take part in those deliberations in open and accessible public fora, and inform or influence decisions. A process which can only occur when councillors act in public, without a pre-decided party whip, enabling those responsible for decisions to be held more readily to account.

The democratic renewal agenda, whilst not fundamentally threatening the representative nature of local democracy, intensifies participatory pressure at the local level. Local government is to remain a key feature of British representative democracy, but its representative nature is to be made more sensitive to the demands of diverse and pluralistic local communities (Gyford, 1986). Local government structures and the councillors that work within them are firmly set in the Burkean mould, that is freedom for the representative from the represented, thus allowing the councillor to focus loyalty on the group – not the community (Eulau et al., 1959; 1978). The democratic renewal formula to ensure local government responsiveness to its citizens, community engagement and improved openness, transparency and accountability, is not the replacement of its representative foundations, but rather enhanced citizen participation and an institutional distinction between the executive and representative/scrutiny roles of the councillor. Thus, democratic renewal offers more liberal democracy rather than fundamental change (Phillips, 1994).

The Party Group and Transparent Local Democracy

Councillors have long recognised that success in council rests on members acting as coherent and disciplined groups; even prior to the 1835 Municipal Corporations Act it was possible to recognise the national party allegiance of members of the unreformed corporations. Indeed, the battle for the new corporations was largely a party battle, fought between Conservatives and Liberals (Fraser, 1979). Moreover, from 1835 candidates for an array of representative bodies have, over time, used a variety of labels to secure election and identify themselves in council (Grant, 1971; Young, 1975; Gyford, 1985). Whilst party politics has been a long-standing element of local government, so too has the group system. What has varied over time and place – and between the parties – is the degree of group coherence and discipline (Birch, 1959; Lee, 1963; Bealey et al., 1965; Clements, 1969;

Jones, 1969; Ellis Jones, 1986; Davis, 1988). Nationally, political parties developed their own approaches to the organisation and activities of councillors, approaches which are open to local interpretations, varying across and within parties (Copus, 1999). Bulpitt (1967), identified that over time the texture of party group activity and organisation had changed, and continues to change – a change resting on the degree to which councillors acted as coherent political groupings to settle patronage and policy issues. Whilst Labour councillors are willing to admit to a rule-driven group loyalty, Conservatives and Liberal Democrats maintain they are less controlled by their group – but they are just as likely to comply. They simply rely more on political culture and a preference for unified action, and less on standing orders and disciplinary procedures (Copus, 1997).

The group system has some advantages: it brings direction, certainty and consistency to council decision making and policy; it encourages councillors to govern the authority as a whole, rather than pursuing what some consider to be narrow and sectional interests emanating from wards or divisions. Councillors work as a group to deliver, or oppose, a policy platform supported by the electorate. With majority control, the group system highlights political responsibility and accountability – albeit in broad terms. The group provides a private, protective environment for councillors to consider complex issues, where options can be considered without public or media outrage clouding political judgement, thus encouraging political experimentation and initiative. Once decisions are taken in group, councillors are expected to adhere to them and so enter committee or council with a known body of support. It is, however, the very nature of party group public coherence that has the potential to generate a collision of views between group and citizenry and result in councillors publicly representing the group rather than the electorate.

Much of the criticism of party politics in local government is misdirected, based on a misinterpretation of parties in council. It is the group system, and not party politics *per se*, which has negative effects on local representation. First, the group hides real political responsibility, and masks individual accountability. Secondly, the group is a closed theatre for deliberation and decision making which excludes the citizen, ensuring that representation and decision making remains secret, diluting transparency, accountability and responsiveness. Thirdly, the group becomes the most important place within which councillors conduct representation, influencing councillors' public behaviour. Fourth, the group system can generate a *crisis of representation* for the councillor, when the demands of group loyalty collide with the demands for local representation, resulting in councillors acting against the wishes of their electorate, or even their own views. Finally, the demands of group loyalty and cohesion may distort new political management processes.

Local government rests on action taken by collective bodies – committee or council – and of accountability resting with those bodies. However, before council and committee takes place, most decisions have already been made by the majority group in private meetings. Political decision making is obfuscated on two levels: first, committee decision making disperses responsibility, making individual accountability almost impossible; secondly, committee (and council) hide the real decision-making processes taking place within the party group. Thus, both the formal and public, council and committee, and the private, informal party group, act in tandem to cloud accountability and obscure political responsibility – rendering much local political decision making opaque. A cumbersome, hierarchical committee structure and the restraints of group discipline and secrecy prevent clear accountability and community leadership (Whitehead, 1997). Moreover, the group system militates against the enhanced openness and public debate necessary for effective scrutiny of a political executive; the party group demands private debate and public unity (Stewart *et al.*, 1998). Committees, however, need not present a problem for transparent local government if used for open deliberation (Prior *et al.*, 1995). Councils' failure to provide a forum for public debate is as much a product of the privacy of the group system as structural weakness inherent in committees.

Group Loyalty and Discipline

The conduct and extent of group discipline is an issue that strikes at the heart of local democracy (Jones and Stewart, 1992). Group loyalty and discipline means that councillors often act differently from how they would act as independent representatives. The group demands loyalty, and the councillor must either comply with or dissent from it – generally groups maintain discipline (Gyford *et al.*, 1989; HMSO, 1986; Young and Davis, 1990). The political parties, through rules and standing orders, encourage councillors to conduct representation within the secrecy of the group rather than open and accessible places, drawing the councillor's loyalty towards the group and away from the community. Thus, the councillor's relationship with the electorate is not such that they interact upon one another in an 'ideal representative system' (Sharpe, 1960). Once decisions are made, the group expects the councillor's public support, or at least avoidance of opposition. That expectation, the disciplinary mechanisms available to ensure compliance, and a 'strict' or 'loose' interpretation of discipline, underpins group coherence (Bulpitt, 1967). Disciplinary action, however, is comparatively rare compared to the regularity with which councillors impose their own self-discipline.

Group loyalty is indicative of an approach to local democracy that stresses party over community representation and open decision making. Loyalty results in councillors acting in public unison, particularly in council and committee, and serves to ensure that, in all but the most exceptional circumstances, councillors do not cross party boundaries by entering single-issue alliances with political opponents. Groups are able to contain within themselves consideration of ward issues, even eliminating their public expression. When such issues do spill into the public arena the councillor is faced with placing locality before party and expressing dissent from the group, or conforming with it, placing group before locality. Most councillors choose the latter, conducting representation in private group meetings; as a consequence, the visibility of decision making is obscured and the electoral legitimacy of local government impoverished (Green, 1981). Moves to open up local political processes fundamentally challenge the dominance of the party group as the body in which councillors make decisions and come to represent, over and above the electorate. Secrecy and councillor loyalty establishes the group as a forum where representation is conducted away from public gaze, in turn enabling the group to influence councillors' behaviour elsewhere.

THE PARTY GROUP AND OTHER THEATRES OF REPRESENTATION

Councillors use the discretion attaching to their office to select from a range of *theatres of representation*. These theatres are either private and closed from public view or publicly accessible, offering visible representation (see Commission for Local Democracy, 1995). The democratic renewal objective of opening up local political decision making so that it becomes transparent and hence more accountable rests on the idea that local democracy must be seen to be done. If local democracy is to be visible councillors must act as representatives and decision makers in those places that are accessible to the public. Indeed, they must eschew the private deliberation and decision making which is at the heart of the group system and of much political activity (Dahl, 1961). The choice councillors make of where and how to act and whether they prefer to act in the open, or in private venues, are issues at the heart of democratic renewal. Thus it is important to explore these preferences. Figure 1 displays the range of theatres where councillors can act, and the acts they can employ.

The closed and open *theatres of representation* have different degrees of secrecy and transparency attaching to them and actions embarked upon in 'closed' settings are not witnessed by the electorate and may differ from those chosen in more open settings. Central to understanding the influence of the group within local democracy is whether councillors display a

FIGURE 1
THEATRES OF REPRESENTATION AND REPRESENTATIVE ACTS

	Speak	Vote	Abstain	Comply	Absent
Open Theatres					
Council	✓	✓	✓	✓	✓
Committee	✓	✓	✓	✓	✓
Public Meeting	✓	✗	✗	✓	✓
Local Press	✓	✗	✗	✓	✓
Electronic Media	✓	✗	✗	✓	✓
Closed Theatres					
Party Group	✓	✓	✓	✓	✓
Local Party	✓	✓	✓	✓	✓
Private meetings	✓	✗	✗	✓	✓

TABLE 1
LIKELIHOOD OF DISSENT: CLOSED THEATRES OF REPRESENTATION

Theatre		Labour % likely	Lib Dem % likely	Con % likely
Party group				
	Speak	93 (221)	99 (99)	93 (220)
	Vote	77 (221)	91 (97)	79 (220)
Party Meeting				
	Speak	92 (223)	95 (97)	88 (214)
	Vote	79 (220)	87 (96)	76 (214)
Private meeting				
	Speak		65	78 79

Note: the base figures are given in brackets

TABLE 2
LIKELIHOOD OF DISSENT: OPEN THEATRES OF REPRESENTATION

Theatre		Labour % likely	Lib Dem % likely	Con % likely
Full Council				
	Speak	25 (218)	59 (97)	62 (218)
	Vote	10 (215)	43 (95)	32 (216)
Committee				
	Speak	38 (220)	66 (97)	72 (218)
	Vote	17 (218)	50 (97)	43 (216)
Public meeting				
	Speak	40 (222)	56 (97)	60 (216)
Local Press				
	Speak	21 (218)	44 (96)	45 (213)
Electronic Media				
	Speak	19 (218)	37 (94)	35 (207)

Note: the base figures are given in brackets

preference for it as a place in which to act and as a body to which they will
be loyal. Tables 1 and 2 display the compressed likely responses from
councillors of the three main parties when asked to indicate how likely they
were to speak or vote against their group in the *theatres of representation* in
Figure 1 when the group faced community opposition.

The Theatres Compared

A clear pattern of representative behaviour and preference for a particular
theatre of representation is discernible from the responses. Councillors
become less likely to act against the group as the theatre of representation
moves outward from the group to increasingly open settings. The councillor,
irrespective of party affiliation, prefers the secrecy of the group, a preference
far more marked for Labour councillors. There is also a correspondence
between the group and the wider political party. It is the privacy and
exclusivity attached to group and party that councillors find conducive to
expressing opposition to the group (see Budge *et al.,* 1972; Game and Leach,
1995). Indeed, councillors are more willing to act as a conduit between the
electorate and the group than the electorate and council chamber.

It is the group as a *theatre of representation* that has the greatest influence
within local democracy. Moreover, the demands of a majoritarian approach
to democracy require the councillor to support or acquiesce to the group in
public however he or she may have acted in group, and whatever articulated
community opinion exists. A point emphasised by a Labour district
councillor who stated: 'you can not keep coming backwards and forwards to
the group with the same subject, you have to let go, democracy is about
accepting defeat, discuss things in group, vote, but then get on with it.'

Councillors distinguish between open theatres of representation
available to them and committee is seen as safer than the council for
speaking and voting. As committee is often less formal, ritualistic and
symbolic than council, acts of defiance of group decisions have less
visibility than in full council. As one Conservative county councillor put it:
'I find it much more comfortable in committee, we have our committee
meetings in a committee room, not the council chamber and you do not feel
quite so on view as you do in the chamber. I am much happier speaking
there, as for voting you say, well I can not see myself voting against the
Conservative group.' Committee can thus offer a venue for open
deliberation should the group system allow – generally, however, it does
not.

Whilst councillors prefer to act in the closed theatres, differences of
degree in willingness to act exist dependent on political affiliation. It is only
the likelihood of such acts which varies between parties; the crucial point at
which political affiliation becomes a determinant of councillor action is in

the shift from closed to open theatres. Here, the Labour councillor is clearly the most reluctant to allow local representation to spill into the public arena.

The group excludes opposition and the community alike from deliberating and deciding local affairs. Whilst councillors view the democratic processes as legitimately conducted in the privacy of the group meeting, reforming political management structures and an institutional distinction between councillors' executive and scrutiny roles will not lead to more transparent and accessible local democracy. That councillors across the political spectrum are predisposed to work within the privacy of the group, rather than open theatres, has important implications for democratic renewal.

COUNCILLORS: A VIEW ON THE ELECTORATE AND A PREFERENCE FOR THE GROUP

Councillors across the political spectrum hold attitudes towards representation and their electorate that stress loyalty to the group rather than the electorate, conflicting with greater public involvement (HMSO, 1986; Copus, 1997). Group discipline and unity are a powerful alternative to demands for representation made by the electorate, an alternative to which councillors are willing to respond. Thus, the group system draws the councillor away from focusing representative loyalty on the community. Whilst councillors generally support an enhanced 'say' for the citizen in local affairs, this is not at the expense of a diminished role for councillors (HMSO, 1986). Councillors can quite rationally indicate they favour more citizen 'say' whilst retaining final decision making themselves. Such decisions, of course, are filtered through the party group.

The Councillor as Local Decision Maker

Councillors were asked to indicate their levels of agreement with the statement: 'It is for local councillors rather than members of the public and pressure groups to make decisions on local needs and priorities.' The statement was drafted to reflect 'community' as a body of opinion,

TABLE 3
'COUNCILLORS SHOULD DECIDE' BY POLITICAL PARTY

Party	Agree strongly	Agree	Neither	Disagree	Disagree strongly	Margin of agreement	Base
	%	%	%	%	%		
Labour	14	43	18	21	4	+32	(222)
Lib Dem	9	44	15	29	3	+21	(98)
Con	29	51	7	12	1	+67	(224)

organised around some purposeful objective, and not the individual citizen seeking generalised input. Table 3 shows responses to the statement.

Councillors firmly believe that they, not the public, should make *decisions* on local issues. A majority of councillors across the parties, including the Liberal Democrats, took this position. Decision making, legitimised by public election, is jealously guarded by councillors. Without it, they have little other than elected office to distinguish them from ordinary citizens. Conservative councillors express more and stronger agreement with this statement and greater support for the councillor as unhindered arbitrator of local affairs.

Enhanced public consultation need not conflict with councillors' decision-making role. Citizen's juries and panels, focus and user groups provide a view of the public mind on issues or priorities; they are in fact perfect vehicles for enhancing citizen 'say' in local affairs. It is the councillor that must negotiate and filter the messages received; thus, the non-binding outcomes of the consultative processes at the heart of democratic renewal need not threaten the councillor as decision maker – only inform that process (Rao, 1993; Young and Rao, 1994; Leach, 1998). It is the group which will be used, much as at present, as a base to counter public criticism and political opposition – often seen by councillors as one and the same. Councillors, however, do not rest on their elected office alone to justify their position as decision maker, they hold strong views about the electorate's parochial interest in local affairs, views which further strengthens the position of the group.

NIMBYISM

Councillors were asked to indicate their level of agreement with the statement: *'people only become interested in local government when an issue directly affects them'*. Table 4 sets out the responses, indicating a clear and worrying scepticism amongst councillors of the motivations of the communities they represent. The clear, conclusive majority of councillors

TABLE 4
'PEOPLE ARE ONLY INTERESTED IN LOCAL GOVERNMENT WHEN AN ISSUE AFFECTS THEM', BY POLITICAL PARTY

Party	Agree strongly %	Agree %	Neither %	Disagree %	Disagree strongly %	Margin of agreement	Base
Labour	25	54	7	12	2	+65	(224)
Lib Dem	29	58	4	8	1	+78	(99)
Con	35	50	6	7	2	+76	(224)

are firmly of the view that the citizenry are primarily motivated by self-interest. There is an overwhelming scepticism amongst councillors towards the electorate they represent, with the attribution of purely self-interested motives reflected in similar proportions across the parties. That scepticism is mutual, mirrored by the unwillingness on the electorate's part to trust councillors to place local interests above those of the party (Young and Rao, 1995). Such mutual scepticism is damaging to the fabric of local representative democracy and sustains councillors' propensity to make the group the focus of representative attention.

THE CONSEQUENCES FOR DEMOCRATIC RENEWAL

The democratic renewal agenda aims to rejuvenate local government, stimulate interest in local political decision making and make visible and accountable those processes which are currently conducted in the privacy of the group room. The party group is not the target of the renewal agenda, but the group and the attitudes of councillors experiencing democracy within it sustain the closed and often unresponsive and unaccountable culture of much local politics. Councillors prefer to act in the privacy of the group, ascribing a legitimacy to it as a forum for deliberation and decision making which is the product of local representative democracy. Councillors are inclined to act as delegates of their group – effectively mandated by private group meetings to act in certain ways in public. Clearly, councillors do not feel bound by the electorate in a similar fashion – acting rather as trustees or politicos, certainly not as delegates of the community (Newton, 1976; Gyford, 1978).

Eulau et al. (1959) distinguished between representative 'style' and 'focus', the former referring to the 'criterion of judgement' used and the latter to a 'geographical unit, a party, a pressure group or an administrative organisation' at the forefront of the representative's attention. In addition, Jones (1975) notes that councillors may 'represent', or focus on, a broad section of the community or individual citizens, an organised group, or another local authority. Such distinctions enable us to gauge whether a councillor is likely to act as a delegate, bound by instructions, a trustee, using personal judgement on issues, or a politico, adopting either approach to suit the political pressures experienced. Moreover, these distinctions tell us whether the representative is a 'party man, a constituency servant, or a mentor' (Rao, 1994). Where councillors place loyalty (or focus) and the approach they adopt toward representation says much for the potential of the democratic renewal project to bring citizens, communities and councillors closer together in the processes of political decision making. Whether the councillor acts as a delegate, politico or trustee, however, it is the group, as a rule-driven organisation with ability to discipline its members, that is best placed to demand the councillor's loyalty. Councillors also enter into a psychological contract with the group, making public acts of disloyalty – such as speaking and voting against the group – seem an aberration (Copus, 1999). Whilst the councillor's attachment to the party group may vary in intensity, representation is still conducted within the group. Thus, even for the councillor with the loosest attachment to party the group is an important decision-making theatre (Corina, 1974).

Across parties, councillors are likely to focus on the group and to act as delegates from, and of, the group, publicly bound by its instructions or decisions. Whilst the councillor may adopt a trustee or politico style in public, if such a style brings the councillor to agree with the group – and in most cases it will – then so much the better. Thus, the group delegate can appear at first glance as a representative that uses his or her judgement to solve complex local problems, when in fact s/he is bound by the decisions of the private group meeting and its collective wisdom. The councillor can focus on locality as a free agent or delegate, but if focused on, and loyal to the group, can adopt only a delegate style, bound by group instructions. Democratic renewal must re-focus councillors away from the group and towards the community and refine representative style so that executive and scrutiny/representative members are clearly seen as tribunes of an electoral area.

As the democratic renewal agenda has so far largely failed to address, in any detail, the party group as the antithesis of the type of local government envisioned, a serious weakness in the renewal project exists. Democratic renewal's reliance on new structures of political decision making and citizen participation will leave largely unchallenged the organisation, processes and practices of party groups. Little will change in local political decision making unless the renewal project adequately addresses councillors' concepts of group loyalty, how councillors conduct representation, their attitudes towards those they represent, their preference for privacy in the political process, and the adherence to a Burkean approach towards representation, seeing the councillor as the final arbiter of local affairs.

The scepticism councillors have about the motivations of citizens for participation raises questions about the way in which councillors will deal with the messages received from the community – particularly if those messages oppose some deeply held belief or political policy. Indeed, councillors often see community opinion as parochial, offending against their wider governing purpose, or party politicise such opinion as organised for, and by, party opponents (Copus, 1997). Enhanced citizen participation increases the opportunity for conflict between councillors and community. The willingness of party groups to use citizen's juries or other democratic renewal paraphernalia is unlikely, and perhaps unwise, when the group has an existing policy to which councillors are expected to adhere in public. As a result, and generally, consultation will occur on those politically safe or uncontentious issues – matters on which a broad political consensus already exists, or where ruling groups do not feel consultation could be used by opponents for political capital. Whilst some groups will be bold and willing to experiment, many will play the consultation processes with much political caution. A caution related to the attitude amongst councillors: as the elected representatives acting within the group, that they, not the wider community, are the final decision makers.

Accountability is not only improved by greater citizen engagement with political decision-making processes but also by greater clarity as to the point of responsibility for those decisions. The emphasis on an institutional distinction between the executive and scrutiny/representative roles of the councillor, however, displays a weakness of the democratic renewal agenda exploitable by the group system. That weakness is in the over-reliance on structures to alter processes, rather than tackling the political culture generated by the group system – a culture which ensures group dominance in local democracy. The question is, how will groups react to the challenge of new political structures to maintain dominance of local democracy, and thus thwart much of the renewal agenda?

The introduction of formal cabinet government, a clear distinction between executive and scrutiny/representative councillors, and enhanced citizen participation challenges current political practices. The very nature of the group system and the extent of group loyalty, coherence and discipline is questioned. Cabinet government, like enhanced citizen consultation, brings its own special threat to the group system, and whilst the executive models within the White Paper will impact on the group in different ways, any change has the potential to reinforce group cohesion and secrecy rather than open-up and make more accountable the political processes (Stewart et al., 1998). The leader and cabinet model is the most likely option to be selected as a political executive as it represents a formalisation of already existing group-dominated political processes. Indeed, it has been estimated that 90 per cent of councils would opt for a leader and cabinet – to minimise change (LGC, 7 Aug. 1998).

Council Leader and Cabinet

At present, the controlling group uses its majority to appoint the council leader and committee chairs. The leader and cabinet model retains group responsibility for appointment to executive office on two levels. First, where a clear majority exists the leader would be elected from that group; secondly, the group could also elect cabinet members and even allocate portfolios. The group forms the council leadership's electoral constituency (as now), and while in the majority will provide the council's political executive. Where a hung council exists, party groups will be required to negotiate in the process of executive forming and as no one group can guarantee its candidate's appointment, groups will experience pressure to maintain unity in support of their nominations.

Once elected, the leader and cabinet may have full group membership; observer, non-voting status; or end their membership of the group, no longer attending its meetings. The relationship between executive and group will be a product of national political parties redrafting group standing orders. Standing orders could bind the executive to the group, treating it in an undifferentiated fashion for the purpose of loyalty and discipline. Thus, the group could discipline the leader and cabinet, effecting compliance with its decisions and, using a range of sanctions, and ultimately refusing to re-elect the leader and cabinet, ensure the group and political executive remain largely as one. Party groups are likely to adopt the leader and cabinet model because it provides greatest potential for maintaining the current influence of the group over the executive – diluting much of the purpose of democratic renewal. The whip, however, could be used more sparingly, applying to the leader and cabinet only when acting as members of the council, making a clear distinction between the role of executive and non- executive councillors.

The leader and cabinet are clearly members of the group; they were elected as such and subsequently appointed to their positions by the group, unlike the directly elected mayor. The power of appointment sets the context for the relationship between executive and group, but is not the most important aspect of that relationship. As the executive will need to govern through the council the voting strength and coherence of the majority group is essential for effective executive activity. Thus, the group can ensure the executive broadly 'executes' group policy. An executive requires a continuous and coherent bloc of support amongst councillors (from the majority party), to ensure its political control. The executive (which has retained its membership of the group) and the group will negotiate a policy package, which will be formally approved by the group. Once satisfied that the package presents its priorities and objectives, the group will support the executive in council, acting as a coherent and unified bloc of members, using its majority to ensure executive policy receives council acceptance. As a result, the need to maintain group cohesion and public unity is intensified and decision making remains a secret process.

The ability of groups to negotiate with and influence the executive, and the executive's need for a bloc of councillors acting in a coherent fashion to support agreed policy, has a fundamental impact on the scrutiny function. Majority group councillors acting in scrutiny committees will be predisposed towards supporting an executive they have appointed and whose policy they have helped formulate. Whilst scrutiny demands that councillors are not whipped, for majority and minority groups, it may require cohesive and sustained action and compliance with pre-meeting decisions. Thus, new models may intensify pressure to maintain public unity; debate and scrutiny remain private, and the group is the prime theatre of representation and the body to which councillors are loyal.

The mayoral models have a greater potential than leader and cabinet for blurring and diluting of party loyalties. Those models demand a freedom from group influence, with the mayor bound by the group for only those decisions which require council – and therefore group – approval, such as the mayoral budget. The demands of party unity, however, the fear of the party appearing divided and the electoral misfortune that is believed to deliver, adds a pressure on parties to minimise the potential for disagreement. Political parties may wish to ensure that the mayor works in concert with the group – thus retaining an important element of group unity and cohesion across executive and council. This is far cry from the group's current power to discipline members and ensure compliance, or indeed its relationship with a leader and cabinet appointed from, and by, the group.

The Party Group

There is no reason to suggest that party groups will radically alter their current arrangements for ensuring group cohesion and unity to meet new political arrangements. Groups will need to act in a unified fashion to secure success in the council chamber; to act effectively against a majority or minority group; to avoid the political embarrassment of damaging public divisions; and, importantly, group cohesion will be essential for supporting or scrutinising a political executive. National parties and their groups will be faced with pressures to loosen the whip to facilitate effective scrutiny. Scrutiny implies the absence of a whip and councillor freedom to act unrestrained by pre-meeting decisions; scrutiny committees could see councillors acting with greater autonomy from the group, but whipped on major policy. A counter-pressure exists, however, where councillors support or oppose an executive depending on party affiliation. In such cases, the tendency is towards group cohesion and pre-planned debate along party lines, maintaining group cohesion against political opponents and executive. How groups change to meet new political management and the demands of transparency will be a product of the same political culture and attitudes towards representation that will lead most groups to opt for the leader and cabinet model – minimal change is likely to the way groups organise and operate.

Where the full council has control over budgetary or major policy issues the party group will doubtless want to determine how its members should act. Little change is likely in full council to the current practices of group pre-meetings, private debate and decision making and application of the party whip. Some loosening of discipline may occur when councillors use full council to act as representatives and raise local issues. Even then, they will need to ensure that local issues do not confront group policy. The blurring of boundaries between local and policy matters and distinctions between executive and non-executive councillors will combine with councillors' preference for conducting business in private to ensure groups maintain private debate and public coherence.

CONCLUSION

National political parties must adapt group rules and standing orders to create the open and transparent culture and environment necessary for effective scrutiny and representation. The challenge in redrafting the relationship between councillor and group is to ensure debate and decision making does not remain closed to the public. Groups could expect adherence to broad political principles; regular attendance at group meetings; public courtesy and respect for party colleagues; the highest standards of probity and integrity in the conduct of council affairs; adherence to the law and codes of conduct; careful balancing of the needs of party unity with the demands of local representation; and a concern for effective group organisation. They should not expect members' unfailing public loyalty and adherence to group decisions, irrespective of councillor's views, and those of local communities. They should no longer expect councillors to act one way in group and another in public as a consequence of group decisions – particularly when conducting their representative or scrutiny function. Two scenarios suggest themselves when considering how groups could respond to the challenges of democratic renewal.

Worst Case Scenario

Where a political culture of secrecy and intense group loyalty exists, the introduction of a leader and cabinet could see the group continue to operate as though nothing had happened. The power of the group would be retained through discipline and expectations of loyalty, but secrecy would be increased through executive decision making, which would remain publicly unscrutinised. Only symbolic scrutiny would occur by majority party back-benchers who had previously discussed and decided upon issues in group. Moreover, existing one-party states would remain intact, with the problems of democratic accountability in such circumstances intensified. Executive and scrutiny councillors could attempt to impose discipline on each other; as members of the same group, it would be convenient to use a party majority – as it is now – to avoid public criticism and for support against the opposition. As a result, local councils with new powerful political executives would be further distanced from the communities they represent and the health of local democracy damaged.

Best Case Scenario

Alternatively, councillors can embrace a new political culture and approach to conducting council affairs. On adopting a new political executive, back-benchers could be freed to play a genuine scrutiny and representative role, even in one-party states, thus removing most of the worst aspects resulting from a lack of political opposition. Public and open deliberation of local issues returns to the council chamber, which regains its importance as a place where councillors consider issues, speak and vote according to their beliefs and the views of those they represent. Council chambers become the place where local democracy is expressed by councillors unfettered by current patterns of group discipline. In these new circumstances groups will still meet to decide broad policy responses to major issues and councillors will support the outcomes of group meetings, not as a result of disciplinary processes, but because they reflect choices based on shared political views. Those that remain unconvinced will be free to express their doubts and vote accordingly. Local democracy becomes more fluid and the outcome of council meetings difficult to predict. Ultimately, however, the health of local democracy is enhanced and the council becomes a genuine representative body, reflecting community concerns and priorities, not the dictates of group meetings.

Stewart *et al.* (1998) indicate that different political management models imply different relationships between executive and party group, and that these relationships largely fall to the political parties to accommodate. Leaving political parties to regulate themselves in such matters may be inappropriate, as the outcome of any review of group procedures could be a retention of the group system in a modified form. The ultimate purpose of new standing orders would be public party unity and cohesion. Thus, the separation of executive and scrutiny functions does nothing to remove the real barrier to transparent, accountable and responsive local democracy – the party group. Moreover, the Green and White Papers (HMSO, 1998) and the draft bill (HMSO, 1999) make only scant reference to the party group whilst attempting to introduce major change to the structures of local government and, via that route, to the influence of the group. The Labour Party nationally has recognised that the culture and practices of the party group must change to meet new political management arrangements (Labour Party, 1999). Yet it appears the government is reluctant, at least in the documentation produced so far, to address that formalised informality that is the party group, in anything other than a coded perfunctory manner.

If the democratic renewal project is to succeed in making local government more transparent, responsive and accountable, changes are required in the way councillors organise and conduct the business of representation through and by the party group. If councillors are to become the advocates or champions of the wards or divisions they represent, then the focus of councillor loyalty must shift from the group to local communities. Simply enhancing opportunities for citizen participation and institutionalising the distinction between executive, scrutiny and representative roles is unlikely to lead to this shift of loyalty. A stimulus is required to encourage large-scale transference of loyalty amongst councillors from the group to the electorate. Perhaps it is time to legislate to control the activities of party groups in whipping members and disciplining them when acting against group decisions. Such legislation would be controversial, raising arguments about encroachment on, and restrictions to, the very institutions by which democracy is made live – political parties – specifically, their manifestation as the party group. Such, criticisms could be countered, however, by reference to the negative impact on representative democracy and open, transparent and responsive local government by the group system.

Democratic renewal is a more subtle process than suggested above, but its subtlety may not be sufficient to alter radically the relationship between the councillor, his or her party group and the electorate. Structural change may introduce a new set of mechanisms for making political decisions and a new type of councillor to make them. The long-term success of democratic renewal, however, will be judged more against its potential to introduce cultural change into confrontational local politics. Several factors combine to make it probable that the group will continue to be a powerful player in local democracy under any new political management arrangements or with enhanced citizen participation: the secrecy of the group system; its impact on the relationship between the councillor and community; its acceptance by councillors as a legitimate decision-making forum; the all-pervasiveness of group within local government; its reach across the theatres of representation; its loyalty-generating expectations; and its linking of local democracy with national politics (see Blondel and Hall, 1967). The challenge is not only to change how councils manage their affairs, but how party groups operate, opening them up to the demands of public scrutiny – otherwise local democracy will remain conducted behind the closed doors of the group room, whatever formal political management systems exist.

REFERENCES

Almond, G.A. and S. Verba, 1963, *The Civic Culture: Political Attitudes and Democracy in Five Nations* (New Jersey: Princeton University Press).

Bealey, F., J. Blondel and W.P. McCann, 1965, *Constituency Politics: A Study of Newcastle-under-Lyme* (London: Faber and Faber).

Bellof, M. (ed.), 1948, *The Federalist Papers or the New Constitution* (Oxford: Basil Blackwell).

Birch, A.H., 1959, *Small Town Politics: A Study of Political Life in Glossop* (London: Oxford University Press).

Blondel, J. and R. Hall, 1967, 'Conflict, Decision-Making and the Perceptions of Local Councillors', *Political Studies*, Vol.15, No.3, pp.322–50.

Budge, I. *et al.*, 1972, *Political Stratification and Democracy* (London: MacMillan).

Bulpitt, J.G., 1967, *Party Politics in English Local Government* (London: Longmans).

Bulpitt, J.G., 1972, 'Participation and Local Politics', in G. Parry (ed.), *Participation in Politics* (Manchester: Manchester University Press), pp.281–302.

Clements, R.V., 1969, *Local Notables and the City Council* (London: Macmillan).

Community Leadership and Representation, 1993, *Unlocking the Potential, The Report of the Working Party on the Internal Management of Local Authorities in England* (London: HMSO).

Cochrane, A., 1986, 'Community Politics and Democracy', in D. Held and C. Pollit (eds.), *New Forms of Democracy* (London: Sage), pp.51–77.

Commission for Local Democracy, 1995, Final Report, *Taking Charge: The Rebirth of Local Democracy* (London: Municipal Journal Books).

Conduct of Local Authority Business, 1986, Committee of Inquiry into the Conduct of Local Authority Business, *Research Vol. I. The Political Organisation of Local Authorities* (London: HMSO).

Conduct of Local Authority Business, 1986, Committee of Inquiry into the Conduct of Local Authority Business, *Research Vol. II, The Local Government Councillor* (London: HMSO).

Copus, C., 1997, 'The Influence of the Political Party Group on the Representative Activities of Councillors' (unpublished Ph.D. thesis, University of London, Queen Mary and Westfield College).

Copus, C., 1998, 'The Councillor: Representing a Locality and the Party Group', *Local Governance*, Vol.24, No.3 (Autumn), pp.215–24.

Copus, C., 1999, 'The Political Party Group: Model Standing Orders and a Disciplined Approach to Local Representation', *Local Government Studies*, Vol.25, No.1, pp.17–34.

Corina, L., 1974, 'Elected Representatives in a Party System: A Typology', *Policy and Politics*, Vol.3, No.1 (Sept.), pp.69–87.

Crick, B., 1982, *In Defence of Politics* (Harmondsworth: Penguin Books).

Dahl, R.A., 1961, *Who Governs?* (New Haven, CT: Yale University Press).

Davis, J., 1988, *Reforming London: The London Government Problem 1855–1900* (Oxford: Clarendon Press).

Davis, J., 1989, 'The Progressive Council, 1889–1907', in Saint, 1989, pp.27–48.

de Tocqueville, A., 1994, *Democracy in America*, ed. J.P. Mayer (London: Fontana Press).

Ellis Jones, P., 1986, *Bangor 1883–1983: A Study in Municipal Government* (Cardiff: University of Wales).

Eulau, H. *et al.*, 1959, 'The Role of the Representative: Some Empirical Observations on the Theory of Edmund Burke', *American Political Science Review*, Vol.53, No.3 (Sept.).

Eulau, H. and J. Whalke, 1978, *The Politics of Representation* (Thousand Oaks, CA: Sage).

Fraser, D., 1979, *Power and Authority in the Victorian City* (New York: St Martin's Press).

Game, C. and S. Leach, 1995, *The Role of Political Parties in Local Democracy* (Commission for Local Democracy, Report No.11, Feb.).

Gillespie, J., 1989, 'Municipalism, Monopoly and Management: The Demise of Socialism in one County, 1918–1933', in Saint, 1989, pp.103–25

Glassberg, A., 1981, *Representation and Urban Community* (London: MacMillan).

Grant, W.P., 1973, 'Non-partisanship in British Local Politics', *Policy and Politics*, Vol.1, No.3, pp.241–54.

Green, D., 1981, *Power and Party in an English City: An Account of Single-Party Rule* (London: Allen and Unwin).

Gyford, J., 1978, *Local Politics in Britain* (London: Croom Helm).

Gyford, J., 1985, 'The Politicisation of Local Government', in M. Loughlin, M. Gelfand and K. Young (eds.), *Half a Century of Municipal Decline* (London: Allen & Unwin), pp.77–97.

Gyford, J., 1986, 'Diversity, Sectionalism and Local Democracy', in Committee of Inquiry into the Conduct of Local Authority Business, *Research Vol. IV, Aspects of Local Democracy* (London: HMSO), pp.106–31.

Gyford, J. and M. James, 1983, *National Parties and Local Politics* (London: Allen and Unwin).

Gyford, J., S. Leach and C. Game, 1989, *The Changing Politics of Local Government* (London: Unwin).

Hampton, W., 1970, *Democracy and Community: A Study of Politics in Sheffield* (London: Oxford University Press).

Held, D., 1993, *Models of Democracy* (Oxford: Polity Press).

Hennock, E.P., 1973, *Fit and Proper Persons: Ideal and Reality in Nineteenth-Century Urban Government* (London: Edward Arnold).

Jones, G.W., 1969, *Borough Politics: A Study of Wolverhampton Borough Council 1888–1964* (London: Macmillan).

Jones, G.W., 1975, 'Varieties of Local Politics', *Local Government Studies*, Vol.1, No.2, pp.17–32.

Jones G.W. and J. Stewart, 1992, 'Party Discipline through the Magnifying Glass', *Local Government Chronicle*, 30 Oct.

Kavanagh, D., 1989, 'Political Culture in Great Britain: The Decline of the Civic Culture', in G.A. Almond and S. Verba (eds.), *The Civic Culture Revisited* (London: Sage), pp.124–76.

Keith-Lucas, B., 1952, *The English Local Government Franchise* (Oxford: Basil Blackwell).

Labour Party, 1999, *Modernising Labour Groups and Local Governance* (London).

Lambert, J., C. Paris and B. Balckaby, 1978, *Housing Policy and the State: Allocation, Access and Control* (London: MacMillan).

Leach, S., 1998, *It's Our Party: Democratic Problems in Local* (London: Local Government Management Board).

Lee, J.M., 1963, *Social Leaders and Public Persons: A Study of County Government in Cheshire since 1888* (Oxford: Clarendon Press).

Local Government Chronicle, 7 Aug. 1998.

Local Democracy and Community Leadership (HMSO, 1998).

Local Leadership: Local Choice (HMSO, 1999).

Manin, B., 1997, *The Principles of Representative Government* (Cambridge: Cambridge University Press).

Marsh, A., 1977, *Protest and Political Consciousness* (London: Sage).

Modern Local Government: In Touch with the People (White Paper, HMSO, 1998).

Muchnick, D., 1970, *Urban Renewal in Liverpool* (Occasional Papers on Social Administration, The Social Administration Trust, London: Bell & Sons).

Newton, K., 1976, *Second City Politics: Democratic Processes and Decision-Making in Birmingham* (Oxford, Clarendon Press).

Newton, R., 1968, *Victorian Exeter* (Leicester: Leicester University Press).

Owen, D., 1982, *The Government of Victorian London, 1855–1899: The Metropolitan Board of Works, the Vestries, and the City Corporation* (Cambridge, MA: Harvard University Press).

Parry, G., G. Moyser and N. Day, 1992, *Political Participation and Democracy in Britain* (Cambridge: Cambridge University Press).

Parry, G., 1977, *Political Elites* (London: George Allen and Unwin).

Phillips, A., 1994, *Local Democracy: The Terms of the Debate* (London: Commission for Local Democracy, Report No.2, June).

Prior, D., J. Stewart and K. Walsh, 1995, *Citizenship: Rights, Community and Participation*

(London: Pitman).

Rao, N., 1994, *The Making and Unmaking of Local Self-Government* (Aldershot: Dartmouth).

Rao, N., 1993, *Managing Change: Councillors and the New Local Government* (York: Joseph Rowntree Foundation).

Saint, A. (ed.), 1989, *Politics and the People of London: The London County Council 1889–1965* (London: Hambledon Press).

Sartori, G., 1962, *Democratic Theory* (Detroit: Wayne State University Press).

Saunders, P., 1979 *Urban Politics: A Sociological Interpretation* (London: Hutchinson).

Schumpeter, J.A., 1974, *Capitalism, Socialism and Democracy* (London: Unwin).

Sharpe, L.J., 1960, 'The Politics of Local Government in Greater London', *Public Administration*, Vol.38, No.2 (Summer), pp.157–72.

Stewart, J. *et al.*, 1998, *Practical Implications: New Forms of Political Executive* (London: Local Government Management Board and Local Government Association).

Stoker, G., 1991, *The Politics of Local Government* (Basingstoke: Macmillan).

Whitehead, A., 1997, *By the People, For the People: Community Governance: Reconnecting Representation and Participation* (London: Local Government Information Unit).

Young, K., 1972, 'Political Party Organisation', in G. Rhodes (ed.), *The New Government of London: The First Five Years* (London: Weidenfeld and Nicolson).

Young, K., 1975, *Local Politics and the Rise of Party: The London Municipal Society and the Conservative Intervention in Local Elections, 1894–1963* (Leicester: Leicester University Press).

Young, K. 1989, 'Bright Hopes and Dark Fears: The Origins and Expectations of the County Councils', in K. Young (ed.), *New Directions for County Government* (London: Association of County Councils), pp.4–21.

Young, K. and P. Garside, 1982, *Metropolitan London: Politics and Urban Change 1837–1981* (London: Edward Arnold).

Young, K. and M. Davies, 1990, *The Politics of Local Government since Widdicombe* (York: Joseph Rowntree Foundation).

Young, K. and N. Rao, 1995, 'Faith in Local Democracy', in J. Curtice *et al.* (eds.), *British Social Attitudes: The Twelfth Report* (Aldershot: Dartmouth).

Young, K. and N. Rao, 1994, *Coming to Terms with Change: The Local Government Councillor in 1993* (York: Joseph Rowntree Foundation).

Political Leadership in the New Urban Governance: Britain and France Compared

PETER JOHN AND ALISTAIR COLE

The tension between leadership and democracy is always implicit in the governance of the contemporary city. The qualities that make local political systems work are the same ones that can undermine the claims of liberal democracy to be an effective and responsive type of government. Yet there are circumstances when strong leadership combines with effective democratic control. In particular, we argue in this paper that there are creative pathways that local political leaders may take to mobilise local communities for collective action; and skilful leaders can raise the governing capacity of local communities. To achieve these contradictory aims, there are a variety of leadership styles that emerge in different contexts, and each has its costs and benefits.

The leadership task is daunting because there is no obvious winning formula, partly because it depends upon a capacity to play many roles, many of which are contradictory. As local chief executives, leaders make executive decisions; but as this involves deciding for or against local interests, they are often unpopular. As public representatives, leaders have a duty to express the unity of the urban space, but also to reflect its diversity. In their role as party chiefs, finally, leaders have to manage their followers in their political parties, and attempt to disarm internal party challenges. In trying to square these circles, it is not surprising that leaders often fail to rise to the challenge.

The travails of the leadership role are accentuated by the character of urban politics. National political leaders are at the natural high point of political systems that claim, if they do not always exercise, sovereignty. Leaders inherit a mantle of legitimate power, with a formidable set of institutions and the ability to manipulate symbols to further their ends. At the urban level, on the other hand, the exercise of power and authority is more ambiguous. The boundaries of urban territories do not have the sanctity of national borders, but they are created by higher tier authorities. They often overlap; usually no single authority can claim to represent the complex urban space in its totality, with its overlapping and imprecise city

Peter John, Birkbeck College, University of London; Alistair Cole, University of Cardiff centres, suburbs and regions. Local leaders can find it hard to be visible in nationalised political cultures. Moreover, the nature of the urban space implies a loose collection of political interests, some of which may not have a location in the exact territory occupied by a local political authority. The challenge for urban leaders is to make sense of the complexity and to bring together a disparate set of potential participants. The tasks of creating the urban space and unifying it can be defeating. The temptation is for leaders to retreat into their bureaucratic citadels or to become patrons of collections of minor clients.

The leadership problem is now more acute because many of the certainties of urban politics have diminished. The stable institutional structures that governed western localities have been replaced by more changeable and shifting frameworks. Local political monopolies have been broken. The number of local political actors and non-elected authorities have increased. Central government departments and agencies play a more important role in deciding local matters than hitherto. The growing importance of the economy in the life of cities and the incisiveness of economic competition have given a new edge to local politics. Economic competition has brought business and many other private actors back into public life. At the same time, growing demands from citizens and interest groups have increased the pressure on local political decision makers. The consequence of institutional fragmentation and the participation of new actors is summarised by the term 'local governance', which implies a more open, flexible and networked pattern of decision making than traditional local government (Stoker, 1997). Local governance removes many of the old contours of governing by multiplying the numbers of actors in local politics, raising the level of complexity of public problems, imposing high costs on policy errors, especially on the economic health of cities, and increasing the speed at which policy problems need to be solved. While fragmentation means that some of these tasks can be loaded off onto other bodies, effective problem solving still rests on the ability of the one person at the centre. In fact, rather than creating decentralised self-managing local policy-making systems, local governance increases the demands made on the occupant of legitimate political authority. Citizens and other local leaders target their attention on political leaders at the very time the burdens of office have increased.

In England, the Labour government that came into office in 1997 responded to these concerns with the proposals, amongst other reforms of the local executive, to create more powerful leaders, mayors that would be directly elected by local citizens (DETR, 1998). The idea is that leaders may be able to give much more coherence to local governance through their more public role and defined powers, a model that has been lifted from more executive dominant systems in the rest of Europe. Yet, as we show through our discussion of how leaders in four cities in Britain and France have responded to the conditions of urban governance, the performance of these leaders depends as much on their context, their capacity and their choices as on their formal powers.

LEADERSHIP ROLES IN THE NEW URBAN GOVERNANCE: A TYPOLOGY

The study of leadership is a multidisciplinary exercise, attracting work in the fields of psychology, management studies, organisational theory and history, as well as from political science. Most attention has centred upon character traits and personal skills; the institutional offices or positions occupied by leaders; the governing and policy environment (or political culture), and the variable dimensions of political leadership, such as supra-national, 'core executive', or local (Rhodes and Dunleavy, 1995; Elgie, 1995; Stone, 1995). The object of leadership studies has ranged from the psychological to the institutional. The first set of factors are psychological-personal. Much intellectual energy has been spent on describing the personality types of the leader and whether certain psychological characteristics (such as an activist or an authoritarian temperament) equate with a capacity for leadership (Barber, 1977; Burns, 1978). The psycho-biographical approach leaves many questions unanswered (Berrington, 1974). At best, this approach illuminates why certain types of leaders suit certain historical situations better than others. Personal character traits are an important facet of an ability to exercise political leadership. The leadership qualities of decisiveness, strength, resolution, risk taking, vision and imagination are differentially distributed, irrespective of wider structural circumstances. Different personal skills are appropriate to varying leadership styles and circumstances. The qualities required for political mobilisation are not necessarily the same as those required for inter-organisational bargaining. Leaders also develop over time as they sometimes acquire or lose their skills.

The second set of factors are institutional. Institutions comprise the legal powers of the office holder, the financial levers which leaders may apply and the framework of organisations within which leaders have to interact. In part, institutions are formed by central government laws and constitutions; in part, they evolve through revisions of norms and conventions. Third, there are party organisation and party system factors. Leaders are at the apex of lines of command and traditions in their parties and have to negotiate and respond to the strategies of other parties. There is no escaping the influence of party politics even in the most presidential local government systems.

Within parties, the analyst can compare hierarchical and less hierarchical parties (Miranda, 1994), and each gives leaders more or less freedom of manoeuvre depending on the circumstances. Party can be a powerful resource, but also a cogent restraint on local leadership. Within local party systems, much depends on whether one party is in power over a long period or whether there is a competitive or a multi-party system. In the former, leaders may be secure in their power; in the latter they have to negotiate and to adapt to remain in office. On the other hand, a secure leader may have more freedom to develop capacity-generating policies.

The fourth factor is the political culture that surrounds the local political system. Some local political cultures have high social capital and foster co-operative forms of governance; others may be less trusting and create less creative forms of politics and administration (Putnam, 1993). On the other dimension, while some political cultures may be deferential and accept authoritarian leadership, others may not, and this difference has an implication for the type of leader that is likely to find favour and determines who becomes successful.

But, as has been shown by this discussion, the four factors (they are not exhaustive) have varying effects. Sometimes strong parties create strong leaders; at other times they create weak ones. The same factors can at different times create good or poor exercises of power. Most importantly, the conditions for the emergence of capacious and imaginative leadership are varied. It is these contingencies that inform the comparative analysis of local political leadership.

Leadership studies are littered with typologies. It would be fruitless to try to capture them all in this paper (for some examples, see Barber, 1977; Kotter and Lawrence, 1974). Instead, taking some inspiration from the ones on offer, the following typology tries to set out the type of leader who is likely to emerge in the conditions of urban governance. There are two dimensions at work. One is the continuum between responsive and directive leaders as implied by the discussion at the beginning of this paper. The other is the difference between leaders who generate capacity and those who are self-regarding in a narrow sense, reflecting the idea that leadership is capable of improving the ability of communities to govern. The continuum is captured by Stone's (1989) distinction between power over and power to. The former is about the narrow exercise of power, the latter is about exercising power so all other actors can exercise their potential. The implication is that some leaders are only capable of dominating others, while others have a greater ability. Even though they may seek to crush their rivals, they are more able to inspire co-operation and increase the ability of cities to solve their problems. The typologies can be combined as shown by Figure 1.

FIGURE 1

TYPOLOGY OF LEADERSHIP ROLES IN THE NEW URBAN GOVERNANCE

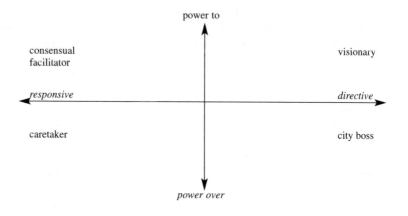

The conditions of governance mean that that leaders are likely to resemble one or a combination of the four roles in this grid. The caretaker is the weak political leader who is unable to manage the complex coalitions that have emerged in local governance. The leader, even if effective as a city manager and as a party chief, finds it hard to cope with the complexity of policy making and the rapidity of policy change. The other type of responsive leader is the consensual facilitator. Just as easygoing as the caretaker counterpart, this leader is far more adaptable and has learnt about the importance of partnerships and networks and keeps abreast of national and local policy debates as they rapidly change. This sort of leader can generate capacity, more by persuasion and finding the best in others than through the efforts and authority of office. The leader is driven along by the reforming efforts of the many partners in local policy making and responds creatively to central initiatives. This type may be initially popular, but finds it hard to develop a coherent local strategy as local policy is driven by the demands of other powerful local actors, the need to please many people at once and to respond to the fashions of the moment.

On the other side of the axis are the strong leaders. The city boss, like the caretaker, does not adapt very well to the new urban governance as the temptation is to retry tough management strategies in conditions where they no longer work. Where an understanding of networking, complex manoeuvring and innovative policy making is required, the city boss does not deliver. Finally, the visionary combines elements of strong leadership with capacity generation. The visionary is the type who can knock heads together, who can break down some of the recalcitrance and divisions in urban politics and who is able to establish more creative policies and effective co-ordination. Complexity is confronted by the will of the leader, who can forge a powerful if disparate coalition. But the cost of this form of capacity generation can be the alienation of the people who do not agree with the vision. The task of the rest of the article is to see what conditions cause the emergence of these types of leader, to evaluate the effectiveness of the regimes that emerge, and to see if there is a tendency for leadership styles to change over time.

THE COMPARATIVE FRAMEWORK

Local diversity is central to the emergence of new governing processes in Europe. First, cities differ greatly in their political traditions, party structures and political cultures even though they operate within the same constitutional structures and national traditions. Leaders emerge in a local milieu that affects who is selected and the ability to command authority. Second, there are variations across nations. Each nation's local government system has its origins at a particular point in history, and has a national constitution, legal framework and a pattern of central–local elite relationships to match (Page, 1991; Page and Goldsmith, 1987). Governance-style restructuring is likely to take different forms across nations and cities, even if there are the common themes of fragmentation and policy change. Different forms of leadership result. The cities we study are in countries that have different political traditions and institutional structures.

Britain

Prior to extensive reforms in the 1980s, British central–local relations were described as deriving from a 'dual polity' (Bulpitt, 1983). Britain's local government system comprised a framework of large local authorities that ran a wide range of services. As local officials and politicians exercised significant legal and financial autonomy from central government, they tended to inhabit a sphere separate from the world of national affairs. Characteristic of the shift from local government, this institutional pattern has been disrupted by a series of central government reforms that have reduced local government discretion, taken away certain functions altogether, created a range of new agencies and set in motion a series of internal reforms of local government management and policy making (Stoker, 1991).

The British leader by tradition lacks visibility and formal power. Rather than holding office, the leader heads the party group, and determines policy through the hierarchy of the political party and the control the party exercises over council business. The legal framework vests power in the elected council and its committees, so it is up to the political party and its leadership to organise council business and to ensure council officers follow its decisions. Leaders are selected by their party groups of councillors. They have to keep the group loyal or else it might vote into power another of its members. Leaders' relationships outside the council are determined by the extent they can act authoritatively and win legitimacy rather than assuming a foreordained role. Some critics suggest the executive is headless and unaccountable because it is unclear who exercises power (see Young, 1994, for a summary of the debate). Other critics believe the leader is too weak and consensual, a tendency that has become more marked over time (Norton, 1978). This finding suggests that British leaders occupy the left-hand side of the quadrant of our table, particularly as, up until 2000, there has been no reform of the office in spite of the massive increase in workload and responsibilities. On the other hand, it is important not to underestimate the power of British leaders. They head large, powerful organisations and they are the most prominent democratically elected individuals in the local area. Moreover, they exercise these resources through relatively disciplined political parties. Indeed, British local politics has had many strong, even ruthless, local political leaders: T. Dan Smith of Newcastle in the 1960s, Herbert Morrison in London in the 1930s and 1940s (Donoughue and Jones, 1973) and John Bradock in Liverpool in the 1940s and 1950s (Baxter, 1972). While leaders became less colourful and powerful in the 1970s, resurgent local public figures emerged during the turbulent 1980s. On the left, there was Ken Livingstone in London, David Blunkett in Sheffield and Ted Knight in Lambeth; on the right, Lady Shirley Porter in Westminster and Paul Beresford in Wandsworth were also powerful and charismatic.

France

Before 1982 the French system of local government was dominated by small, fiercely independent communes, supervised by a powerful and administratively decentralised state in the form of central departments, field agencies and prefectures. In general, the communes did not provide many services and the field agencies provided such functions as roads and education. The complex pattern of administration was characterised by many cross-cutting networks of relationships (Crozier, 1963; Crozier and Thoenig, 1975; Crozier and Friedberg, 1977), and the principal ones were between elected politicians (usually mayors) and state officials (generally prefects and their officials). At any given level, such relations were unequal, since one partner dominated the other, with bureaucratic actors tending to dominate the political ones. Power was exercised with caution since the subordinate partner could always mobilise resources by appealing for support from higher placed representatives of political or administrative authority. After the decentralisation reforms of 1982, the communes acquired more functions, the administrative departments were democratised and elected regions were created. At the same time, some of the strict legal controls over local government were relaxed.

The local leader in France is the mayor, who is directly elected by the public and is also an official of the central state, with laid down duties and responsibilities. In the pre-1982 period, the mayors were powerful because they often had national electoral mandates and an array of central government contacts whereby they could override the initiatives of field officials. They were at the centre of networks of clients in their areas and sought close contact with the prefects (Worms, 1966; Kesselman, 1972; Gremion, 1976). The rise of the big city mayor has been the most notable feature of the new French urban governance. No longer are they primarily subordinate actors. Across France, mayors placed themselves at the head of development coalitions, mobilising large-scale public and private resources to engage in ambitious development projects.

It is much more difficult for a French party to dislodge a mayoral incumbent than in the UK. This can lead to the creation of mayoral dynasties, whereby the local political party becomes an appendage of the town hall, which is central for the distribution of local patronage. French mayors enjoy the legitimacy of direct election. They also select other political personnel: the mayor determines who occupies the powerful position of assistants (*adjoints*), a decision invariably ratified by the first meeting of the new municipal council, and the mayor is usually assisted by a series of offices (*cabinets*). Mayoral patronage extends well into the local administration.

However, the new institutional and political environment has its costs as well as benefits. If local politics was always complex, French-style governance trends have magnified the problem. Institutional proliferation has led to the creation of new tiers of government. New policy problems have produced new coalitions characteristic of urban governance, notably those involving quasi-private sector actors (Lorrain, 1987; 1991). The delegation of responsibly to other actors, such as *adjoint* mayors, creates a problem of control. At the same time, local political leaders have had to respond to a greater number of central initiatives. The problems of leadership have grown, and leaders have had to develop strategies to cope with the pressures (Borraz, 1994; 1998).

COMPARING LOCAL POLITICAL LEADERS

We examined local political leadership in four cities, two each in Britain and France. We selected four different cities: two large metropolitan centres

(Leeds and Lille) and two medium-sized provincial cities (Southampton and Rennes) to show how local political leadership is shaped in part by the specific political, cultural and institutional heritage of each locality. In the ensuing section, we appraise varying patterns of local political leadership in the four cities, with particular reference to the typology outlined above.

Leadership in Leeds

Leeds is one of the major English cities, has a population of just less than 800,000 and is the administrative centre for the region of Yorkshire and Humberside. It is a compact city that has thriving financial, insurance and legal service sectors which all grew rapidly during the 1980s. The city has had a long tradition of powerful civic leadership, typical of Victorian city pride (Briggs, 1963). Since 1980 Leeds has had two relatively long-serving Labour leaders. The first was George Mudie, council leader until 1989, subsequently MP for Leeds East. He was a former NUPE union official, an able administrator and had a reputation for ruthlessness. He ruled Leeds with an iron hand. Under Mudie's leadership all policy and most operational matters were decided by him and a small group of trusted officers. He dispensed with the post of chief executive as he largely carried out this function himself. This directive style of political management ensured that local councillors outside the ruling cabal had little input. Mudie was the traditional boss politician, practised a clientelistic form of politics to stay in power and had limited policy aims. The relative failure of various property regeneration projects (notably the Kirkstall valley scheme) showed the difficulty Mudie faced when seeking to foster consensus and exposed the weakness of his belief that he could impose acceptance of his policies. His period in office demonstrated the limitations of strong personal rule in conditions of local governance.

Jon Trickett was leader from 1989 to 1996. Trickett pursued a very different agenda to Mudie and had a distinct political style. He was an interesting blend of old and new. He adopted more progressive ideas, such as on transport, women's and green issues and local economic development policy, while he was still supported by the old-guard Labour Party which had been so effectively run by Mudie. Trickett believed in partnership with other actors and aspired to be leader of the city, not just of Leeds city council. Even though Trickett modified and professionalised the decision-making process in the council, in essence it was the same pattern established by Mudie. Power in the organisation flowed from the leader, with the officers very much subordinate to him. While he changed the type of policies Leeds pursued, the practice of leadership remained the same. One reason for the concentration of power was because a local authority the size of Leeds City Council needs a powerful figure to pull such a potentially unwieldy organisation together. Cultural reasons were also important; Leeds produces strong leaders because of its traditions of deference and the toughness needed to survive its politics.

Leadership in Lille

Lille is the principal city in northern France. It is a densely populated urban agglomeration reminiscent of British northern cities, with their manufacturing traditions and problems of industrial decline. The Lille Urban Community (CUDL) is fragmented into an inter-authority grouping of 85 communes. Because of its size and centrality, the commune of Lille (172,149 inhabitants in 1990) is the principal town within the Lille Urban Community, and its leader has been the dominant politician in the area. But Lille has never been able completely to dominate its hinterland.

Lille has traditionally produced strong leaders. Pierre Mauroy, who took office in 1973, derived his power from both his position as a classic political *notable* and from his awareness of the governance opportunities in the 1980s and 1990s. In the style of a *notable*, Pierre Mauroy accumulated functions and offices: mayor of Lille, prime minister from 1981 to 1984, senator, Socialist Party leader from 1988 to 1992, and as president of many para-public agencies and development associations. Upon leaving the premiership, Mauroy continued to use his national connections to influence local policy outcomes. Mauroy occupied a central position at the core of local and regional networks: the former premier was pivotal in the wider Socialist network within the Nord/Pas-de-Calais region, which at its height comprised the regional council, the two departmental councils (Nord and Pas-de-Calais) and several large towns. The effectiveness of this pivotal role lessened after 1992, as the Socialist Party (PS) position weakened.

Mauroy also displayed an acute awareness of the need to build governing capacity and to forge alliances with private and voluntary sector interests. Closer co-operation between the Socialist town hall and local economic interests formed an important part of his leadership strategy. Mauroy was the driving force behind this new alliance. He played a highly personal role in promoting major economic development projects such as the international rail link, the new train station and the Euralille commercial and business complex. Without his extensive personal contacts within the public and private sectors, it is uncertain whether the massive Euralille redevelopment project would have proceeded.

The structure of opportunities and the local political culture promoted strong but restrained leadership. The tense relationship between the leading commune Lille, and the urban community (CUDL) paralysed any concerted local economic development strategy for most of the period following the CUDL's creation in 1968. Since 1989, the management of the CUDL has been underpinned by a principle of reciprocity; the large players have tolerated Mauroy's presidency of the CUDL in exchange for a distribution of resources between the leading towns and territorial interests in the metropolitan area. This demonstrates that there are countervailing forces at play; local political leadership needs to be strong to overcome parochial loyalties, but has to be bargained and restrained.

Leadership in Southampton

With a population of 190,000 Southampton is a small city. Its identity was focused first on the port, later on the expansion of firms in the post-war years. Partly because of its quiet character, unclear geography and good communication links, the city lacks a strong cultural and political identity, a factor which limits the possibilities for effective local leadership. Yet when Labour was elected into office in 1984, there followed eight years of activism under the charismatic leadership of Alan Whitehead, supported by a dynamic leadership group. Economic development, based on the positive involvement of business, was central to Whitehead's approach. The Labour council became imbued with the development-orientated spirit of the times, actively courting the involvement of business interests in formulating an economic development strategy, and promoting better inter-organisational relationships. This reflected Whitehead's open style of leadership, which the local business community liked. Whitehead demonstrated considerable political skill in squaring his close relationship with the business community and property developers with a local Labour Party prone to factionalism and the influence of radical groups. The key to Whitehead's strategy was a property-led regeneration on the back of the 1980s economic boom. On the basis of proposals from developers, the council released land and granted planning permission, tried to ensure planning gain for public amenities, and, central government financial rules permitting, used any extra money to fund other public–private projects. Yet Southampton, like many UK cities, does not have enough of a financial or national power base to follow through the larger schemes. The city's experience also showed the limited powers of UK local leaders who have to use complex public–private deals to get projects off the ground. The virtuous circle depended on property-led economic development opportunities, so at the end of the boom years project successes became less common and this affected the buoyancy of the administration. The schemes were also more difficult to pull off as many of the leadership cohort had retired from politics. UK local political leaders are not as able to mobilise national and local actors behind *grands projets* as their French counterparts.

Southampton could not fill the vacuum left by Whitehead's retirement from local politics in 1992. The Labour group became weak and ineffective.

For a while the Liberals took over, then the Labour Party returned in 1994, under the leadership of John Arnold. Arnold provided unassuming and competent leadership. However, he lacked Whitehead's public persona, and co-operation with business, public agencies and neighbouring local authorities remained understated.

Leadership in Rennes

Rennes is a city of 200,000 inhabitants, whose population increases to 333,000 when incorporating the Rennes urban district, an association of 33 communes. The commune of Rennes dominates the Rennes urban district. As mayor of Rennes since 1977, and president of Rennes district after 1989, Edmond Hervé combines elements of old-style political notability with an awareness of the need to develop wider governing relationships. A PS deputy (1978–86, 1988–93, 1997–) and a former health minister, Hervé attempted to exercise influence to ensure favourable central decisions for Rennes.

Rennes' leaders have boasted an original model of local governance. The Rennes model had several reinforcing features: an ideological consensus between local elites to promote the city's economic development and to achieve social progress; a strong mobilisation of new social groups organised into voluntary associations with an input into policy making; the pervasive influence of a progressive Christian-Democratic tradition, expressed through para-Catholic associations; and an innovative style of public sector management, based on long-term urban planning, and municipal intervention (Le Galès, 1993). As in Lille, there is a legacy of strong local political leadership; there have been only two mayors since 1953, the Christian-Democrat Freville, and the Socialist Hervé. Moreover, there has been a large measure of continuity between the two.

Municipal policy was largely consensual throughout the 1980s, but changed somewhat during the third Hervé municipal term after 1990. Whereas political and business elites have moved closer in Lille, the reverse appeared to occur in Rennes during Hervé's third municipal term. Relations between political leaders and representatives of local business deteriorated as a result of two policy initiatives. The first was the 1992 decision to levy the business tax (*taxe professionnelle*) at the level of Rennes district, rather than the 33 individual communes; the second was Hervé's determination to proceed with the VAL, the city metro. After Hervé's decisive victory in the 1995 municipal election, there were signs of a lessening of tension and a revival of the older Rennes model of consensual governance.

FIGURE 2

LEADERSHIP ROLES IN LEEDS, LILLE, SOUTHAMPTON AND RENNES

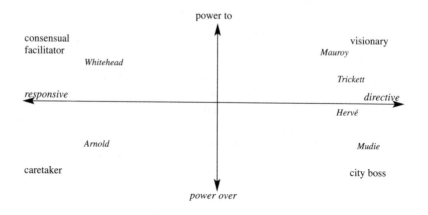

THE LEADERS COMPARED

Applying the typology based on the two dimensions, Figure 2 places the six leaders in the quadrants, with the proviso that leadership is a complex task and involves playing many roles. Consistent with the idea that local governance varies according to place and country, the four cities have produced different types of leader. Most distinctive is George Mudie, who was a city boss. Limited in his policy goals, he was unable to forge a policy learning coalition so necessary in the environment of local governance. His period of office is evidence that new leadership styles are necessary to make local governance work. At the other end of the spectrum is John Arnold, similar to Mudie in that he is an old-style politician, but of the consensual type. As a caretaker, he has adapted better to the new urban governance than his stronger northern counterpart, but there has not been much innovative policy and new forms of co-operation. Next up the scale is Hervé who, at various times in his long political career, has forged an effective governing coalition in Rennes. He tends to rule his patch effectively, but edges towards the directive end of the scale, particularly in later years when his natural political authority waned. His conflicts with business and public sector actors limited his ability to be a capacity generator, though if the graph had been drawn ten years previously he would have crossed over the line. Next up the capacity generating scale is Trickett. In line with the tradition of Leeds politics, he is a strong leader. But in spite of his toughness he is a capacity generator. His vision and belief in partnership created a fresh form of governance in Leeds, which threw off, for a while, the conservative and inward-looking mentality of Leeds' governing culture. Next is Alan Whitehead, who is the classic networking and adaptive politician. He had a vision for the city and sought to improve its pattern of government. He tried to involve many partners in local decision making, and responded to events rather than imposing a firm stamp upon them. Finally, the politician who created the most in the new urban governance was Pierre Mauroy. He managed to use the new freedoms in urban politics and the challenge of an economic crisis to overcome some of the ingrained and bitter political disputes in the Lille metropole.

Institutional factors play a part in explaining the variation of leadership patterns. The French leaders, particularly if they are powerful at the national level, have far more resources and abilities to generate a creative form of politics, and even just to stay in power. It is no coincidence that the two French leaders have both been in office for over 20 years, whereas the most the English politicians managed was nine (see Table 1). The length in office of the mayors reflects their power and allows them to shape local politics. Their achievements, whether it is the new metro in Rennes or the Euralille development complex, owe much to their public prominence and legitimacy, both nationally and locally. English politicians do not have such resources, and their achievements were more limited. Alan Whitehead, who aspired to be a dynamic local leader, failed in many of his schemes. English local political leaders tend to be 'time limited'. For a while they can achieve many real successes, building new partnerships and launching ambitious development schemes. Yet they find it hard to survive in the long term. They lack the political armour and support available to important French local politicians. They do not have a direct democratic mandate; they are not visible to the public; they lack national standing; they have to placate their local parties for fear of being removed in a back-bench coup; the organisations they command are fractured into warring service bureaucracies; there is no cadre of adjoint or deputy mayors doing the leader's bidding; and the financial rewards are minimal for what is a full-time job. The option of becoming a national representative in parliament at the same time as holding local office is not really open. The political tradition of multiple office holding has declined. The divisions between national and local politics and the demands both make in terms of time mean that local politicians often sever their roots. Thus George Mudie, Jon Trickett and Alan Whitehead all stood down as local leaders to fight and to take up parliamentary seats. The question for the English experience is whether such practices are embedded in party politics and the pattern of central–local government relationships, or whether the move towards full-time elected mayors can overcome these systemic limitations.

TABLE 1

LENGTH IN OFFICE OF THE SIX LEADERS

Leader	Term of office	Years in office
Pierre Mauroy	1973–	26
Edmund Hervé	1977–	22
George Mudie	1980–1989	9
Alan Whitehead	1984–1992	8
Jon Trickett	1989–96	7
John Arnold	1994–	5

Yet institutions tell only part of the story. Political parties are important. The moderate but well-organised Labour Party in Leeds produced strong leaders. The clientelistic style of politics ensured leaders could depend on the loyalty of party activists, provided the various territorial factions were pacified. In the Southampton area, the Labour Party is less established, was not so used to governing and was more ideological. As a result it was hard to manage the warring factions within it. Whitehead was skilful in balancing out these elements, and was helped by his chameleon-like political instinct, which, for example, allowed him to be an environmentalist to green activists and to be an expansionist economic developer to the private sector. But even Whitehead's abilities could not in the end prevent his fall from favour. He could not keep pleasing everyone all the time.

Party political constraints are much weaker in the French case; only the electorate can usually force an incumbent leader to quit office. The examples of Lille and Rennes illustrate the municipal basis of French party organisation: even where party federations were strong, as in Lille, they existed in a dependent or subordinate relationship to the municipal authority. As the Rennes example demonstrates, party factionalism could be a potent force during election periods, but did not usually threaten the longevity of municipal leaders. In Lille, the decline of the PS after 1992 limited Mauroy's power, though the mayor of Lille was able to hold on to the CUDL by skilfully managing a complex political framework.

Political culture influenced local leadership. It is no accident that both Mudie and Trickett were strong leaders; while Whitehead and Arnold were more conciliatory. Leeds' culture is hierarchical and deferential, where powerful local elites mutually reinforce each other and wield power in a well-defined context. The power politics of the northern city ensures that only the most ruthless can survive. The culture of Southampton is much less clear, and is more outward focused. Our French examples demonstrate both that leadership patterns can be embedded in local cultural influences; but also that innovative leaders can rise above the conditions of their localities. In Rennes, the capital city of Brittany, there was much continuity in post-war municipal management. Hervé built on the tradition of powerful interventionist mayors. In Lille it was a measure of the skill of Mauroy that he succeeded in imposing a metropolitan vision.

Whatever the institutional, party and cultural constraints, the character and abilities of the individuals in office affected the practice of leadership. The personality of the leader makes a great difference to local decision making (Stone, 1995). In particular, the changed conditions, characterised by the term 'governance', offered challenges. For some, the new complexity and fast-moving environment exposed their limitations. Old patterns of management and political control simply did not work, and they did not adapt well to the new politics. Mudie, Arnold and even Hervé seem to be in this category. For others, local governance was an opportunity to demonstrate their political skills and allowed their personalities full play. Thus the dynamic reputation of Southampton in the 1980s owed much to Alan Whitehead's energy, intelligence and willingness to champion new ideas, and in the readiness of council officers, other local politicians and local elites to follow him in his projects and schemes. Trickett, even without a great deal of public charisma, also supplied an energy and freshness to Leeds' politics. Within the constraints of a tight party machine, a traditional local authority and a parochial local political culture, he did much to open up Leeds and to modernise its policies. Most credit is due to Pierre Mauroy who had the ability and skill to overcome the intense factional politics of the Lille metropole, to build a new alliance with business in spite of decades of political hostility, and to create innovative economic development projects. A lesser leader would have not achieved so much.

CONCLUSION

Leadership is crucial to the new urban governance. The politics of decentralisation, networks, participation, partnerships, bureaucratic reform, rapid policy change and central intervention need powerful but creative figures to give a direction to local policy making. In a time of institutional fragmentation and complexity, leaders make the shifting framework of individuals and organisations work together. They can recreate local identities and senses of purpose in an age where locality has lost its association with traditional industries and well-defined spaces of economic activity. While creating the need for better leadership, the transition to governance imposes intense strains on the people who exercise policy choices. They have to make sense of the complexity and to cope with rapid change and novel circumstances.

The institutional structures, the forms of party organisation and competition and local political cultures count in that they foster certain types of leader, whether directive or responsive, and they offer varied opportunities for leaders to generate governing capacity. Some parties and cultures create an authoritarian form of politics; others encourage more consensual and more co-operative types of behaviour. The French pattern of leadership, operating in its political culture and state tradition, seems to offer more possibilities for creativity by giving mayors extensive resources and a source of legitimacy from the electorate. The interchange between central and local politics by joint office holding reflects the intense localism of French society embedded in the centralised state, and such a culture exists far less in Britain.

The mode of election is also important. Through their position at the head of their party's list, local mayors are almost directly elected. This allows them to claim a local mandate and protects them from faction fighting in their parties. Thus in 1995, after a period when both leaders had taken many political and policy risks, both Mauroy and Hervé were able to face the electorate with their record and to win decisively at the polls. Had Alan Whitehead been an MP as well as local leader, and had he been elected directly by the public, he may have continued his innovative local policies and avoided his retreat in 1992. In spite of the value of direct election, however, the lesson of our research is that the move to elected mayors in Britain will not automatically produce imaginative and creative leaders. They will emerge from their local party and cultural contexts, they will resemble former leaders and only gradually start to use their powers and to forge a new identity. Moreover, the success or otherwise of political leadership owes much to chance combinations of events, to the personality of the protagonists, to the development of political experience, to changing local opportunity structures and to the willingness to risk and experiment.

NOTES

We are grateful to the Economic and Social Research Council for support for the project, 'Local policy networks in Britain and France', grant no L311253047, part of the council's local governance programme.

REFERENCES

Barber, L., 1977, *The Presidential Character: Predicting Performance in the White House* (Englewoods Cliffs, NJ: Prentice Hall).
Baxter, R., 1972, 'The Working Class and Labour Politics', *Political Studies*, Vol.20, No.1, pp.97–107.
Berrington, H., 1974, 'The Fiery Chariot: British Prime Ministers and the Search for Love', *British Journal of Political Science*, Vol.4, No.3, pp.345–69.
Borraz, O., 1994, 'Mayoral Leadership in France', in O. Borraz *et al.* (eds.), *Local Leadership and Decision-Making* (London: LGC for Joseph Rowntree Foundation), pp.11–32.

Borraz, O., 1998, *Gouverner Une Ville Besançon 1959–1989* (Rennes: Presses Universitaires de Rennes).

Briggs, A., 1963, *Victorian Cities* (Harmondsworth: Penguin).

Bulpitt, J., 1983, *Territory and Power in the United Kingdom* (Manchester: Manchester University Press).

Burns, J.M., 1978, *Leadership* (New York: Harper & Row).

Crozier, M., 1963, *Le Phénomène Bureaucratique* (Paris: Seuil).

Crozier, M. and J.-C. Thoenig, 1975, 'La régulation des systèmes organisées complexes', *Revue Française de Sociologie*, Vol.16, No.1, pp.3–32.

Crozier, M. and E. Friedberg, 1977, *L'Acteur et le Système* (Paris: Seuil).

DETR, 1998, *Modern Local Government: In Touch with the People* (Cm 4014, TSO).

Donoughue, B. and G. Jones, 1973, *Herbert Morrison, Portrait of a Politician* (London: Weidenfeld and Nicolson).

Elgie, R., 1995, *Political Leadership in Liberal Democracies* (London: MacMillan).

Giblin-Delvallet, B., 1990, *La Région: territoires politiques. Le Nord-Pas-de-Calais* (Paris: Fayard).

Gremion, P., 1976, *Le Pouvoir Péripherique* (Paris: Seuil).

Kesselman, M., 1972, *Le Consensus Ambigu* (Paris: Cujas).

Kotter, J.P. and P.R. Lawrence, 1974, *Mayors in Action: Five Approaches to Urban Governance* (New York: Wiley).

Le Galès, P., 1993, *Politique Urbaine et Développement Local* (Paris: L'Harmattan).

Lorrain, D., 1987, 'Le grand fossé? Le débat public privé et les services urbains', *Politiques et Management Public*, 3–5 (Paris), pp.83–102.

Lorrain, D., 1991, 'Public Goods and Private Operators in France', in R. Batley and G. Stoker (eds.), *Local Government in Europe* (Basingstoke: Macmillan), pp.89–109.

Miranda, R., 1994, 'Containing Cleavages: Parties and other Hierarchies', in T.N. Clark (ed.), *Urban Innovation: Creative Strategies for Turbulent Times* (Thousand Oaks, CA: Sage).

Norton, A., 1978, 'The Evidence Considered', in G.W. Jones (ed.), *Political Leadership in Local Authorities* (Birmingham: Institute of Local Government Studies).

Page, E.C., 1991, *Localism and Centralism in Europe* (Oxford: Oxford University Press).

Page, E. and M. Goldsmith, 1987, *Central and Local Government Relations* (London: Sage).

Putnam, R., 1993, *Making Democracy Work* (Princeton, NJ: Princeton University Press).

Rhodes, R.A.W. and P. Dunleavy, 1995, *Prime Minister, Cabinet and Core Executive* (Basingstoke: Macmillan).

Stoker, G., 1991, *The Politics of Local Government* (Basingstoke: Macmillan).

Stoker, G., 1997, 'The Economic and Social Research Council Local Governance Programme: An Overview', *Frontières*, 9, pp.15–36.

Stone, C., 1989, *Regime Politics Governing Atlanta 1946–1988* (Lawrence, KS: University Press of Kansas).

Stone, C., 1995, 'Political Leadership in Urban Politics', in D. Judge, G. Stoker and H. Wolman (eds.), *Theories of Urban Politics* (London: Sage).

Worms, J.-P., 1966, 'Le prefet et ses notables', *Sociologie de Travail*, 8, pp.249–75.

Young, K., 1994, 'Local Leadership and Decision-Making: The British System Reconsidered', in O. Borraz *et al.* (eds.), *Local Leadership and Decision-Making* (London: LGC for Joseph Rowntree Foundation).

Rebuilding Trust in Central/Local Relations: Policy or Passion?

VIVIEN LOWNDES

The concept of 'trust' has become central to New Labour's discourse. Renewing trust between *central and local government* is seen as vital in establishing a new and productive working relationship, replacing the suspicion – even downright hostility – which characterised most transactions under previous Conservative administrations. Renewing trust between *local communities and local councils* is seen as fundamental not just to the future health of local democracy but to the government's wider project of 'modernising' the British constitution. Where the Conservative government sought to recast the essence of local government in terms of efficiency or 'value for money', Labour sees renewed trust between councils and communities as a core goal of local government reform. An ambitious programme of 'democratic renewal' aims to rebuild citizens' trust in governance.

Despite an initial atmosphere of anticipation and good will, tensions have emerged in central/local relations. It has become increasingly clear that the government sees trust in central/local relations as emerging out of a 'bargain'. If local authorities can prove they are reconnecting with local communities and promoting service standards, *then* they can be trusted with new powers and enhanced discretion. For its part, local government sees the key to rebuilding trust in central/local relations as a reconfirmation of the principle of local self-government, accompanied by appropriate new powers. To paraphrase the political philosopher John Dunn (1993: 641), trust is for central government a 'policy', while for local government it is a 'passion'. These different understandings are producing a 'chicken and egg' situation that threatens to undermine the broader democratic renewal agenda. Local authorities feel that they have only limited opportunities to change their ways of working without the loosening of central controls (particularly over finance). At the same time, central government argues that local authorities must 'earn' such increased autonomy through demonstrating their willingness and ability to work in new ways.

Vivien Lowndes, De Montfort University

The article is divided into three parts. The first part considers why trust has assumed a central place in discussions of future patterns of governance, exploring the various ways in which the concept has been used. The second part examines the extent to which developments since May 1997 signal a renewal of trust in central/local relations. The third part discusses the tensions that have emerged to threaten the much vaunted 'partnership' ideal, exploring the dynamics of the 'democracy for discretion' bargain that appears to be emerging.

UNDERSTANDING TRUST

The Case for 'More Trust'

There is a renewed interest in 'trust' among politicians, academics and a broad spectrum of social and economic commentators. This interest is as much prescriptive as descriptive. While linked to an analysis of key trends in social, political and economic life, the new importance accorded to trust is highly normative. More trust is considered a 'good thing' – a cornerstone of 'good governance', better management, more sophisticated business relations, and a more sustainable and civilised social and cultural life. The current preoccupation with trust can be illustrated with reference to four key debates, all of which inform the agenda for democratic renewal and modernisation in local government.

Building 'social capital'. Putnam has defined social capital as referring to 'the features of social life – networks, norms and trust – that enable participants to act more effectively to pursue shared objectives' (Putnam, 1995). Strategies to develop social capital are potentially of great importance in addressing social exclusion, reducing citizens' dependence on the state, and revitalising formal democratic processes. There is a link with the 'communitarian' philosophy associated with both the Clinton and Blair administrations that stresses the *responsibilities* as well as the rights of individual citizens (Etzioni, 1995; Tam, 1997). The challenge of fostering bonds of trust among often diverse and conflictual communities is at the heart of the debate about social capital, and a key challenge for local authorities in building the 'community leadership' role at the heart of the government's vision for democratic renewal (see Stoker, 1999: 8).

New forms of competition. From the early 1980s, interest has grown in the potential advantages to business of longer term inter-firm relationships, which are based upon trust, mutuality and shared learning. 'Co-operative competition' stands in stark contrast to the conventional wisdom of formal contracts, secrecy and price bargaining. It is argued to offer gains including risk sharing; access to markets, technologies and complementary skills; shortened innovation cycles; and enhanced learning (Powell, 1996). The replacement of compulsory competitive tendering with 'Best Value', and the promotion of partnership working, represent a clear attempt to ensure that local authorities capture the benefits from what Best (1990) calls 'the new competition'.

New forms of organisation and management. Building trust is increasingly seen as fundamental to good management *within* organisations, as well as across organisational boundaries. Networks can be viewed as an organisational 'third way' – between hierarchical bureaucracies and market-style relationships (Powell, 1991; Lowndes and Skelcher, 1998). Trust, it is argued, constitutes the central organisational glue within networked organisations. Trust 'lubricates' economic exchange and organisational transactions of all sorts; it reduces the costs of communication and relationship building, and facilitates risk taking and innovation (see Granovetter, 1992). The 'business case' for fostering relationships of trust bolsters the moral argument. As Creed and Miles (1996: 35) explain, 'As is often the case, variables such as trust only gain major attention when they move from the category of ethical "oughts" to the category of "economic musts"'. The government's requirement for public consultation as part of the process of establishing Best Value represents a challenge to local authorities to capture both 'managerial' and 'democratic' gains from trust.

Searching for a new governing code. Rhodes argues that ongoing processes of 'institutional differentiation and pluralisation' within government demand the development of a 'new governing code' – neither administrative fiat nor a reliance on quasi-markets will suffice:

> The government will have to learn to live with policy networks, but its toolkit of controls was designed to for an era of line bureaucracies ... The challenge is to understand the new networks and devise ways not only of steering them, but also of holding them to account. (Rhodes, 1997: 110)

Trust is essential for co-operative behaviour within the emerging networks of governance (Rhodes, 1999: xx). Renewed trust between central and local government is likely to be an important element of any new, more appropriate governing code. However, building trust *throughout* the new networks of governance requires the weaving together of different strands of New Labour's 'modernising' agenda – 'democratic renewal' within local government, 'joined up government' to link the myriad of relevant agencies, and higher 'standards' throughout public life.

Trust: The Fundamentals

Having established the importance for local government of broad debates about trust, it is important to explore the fundamental character of the relationships to which we are referring. What is it that constitutes 'trust'? The concept has both an inter-personal (or inter-organisational) aspect, and a more general social or system-wide quality. Hence, trust refers both to:

- the specific expectation that another's actions will be beneficial rather than detrimental to one's own interests (Gambetta, 1988), and

- the generalised ability to 'take for granted, to take under trust, a vast array of features of the social order' (Garfinkle, 1967, cited in Creed and Miles, 1996: 17).

Thinking about central/local relations, trust might thus refer to the expectations that central and local government have regarding the effects (and motivations) of each other's actions, and to the degree of acceptance by both parties of the underlying 'rules of the game'. The greater the level of trust, the less the need for negotiation over matters of detail (and hence a reduction in 'friction' or transactions costs) and the greater the opportunity for long-term planning, risk-taking and innovation. As Meyerson *et al.* (1996: 179) explain: 'Without trust, risk is avoided, innovative activities dry up, only routine actions are available ... and uncertainty remains unresolved'. In situations of uncertainty – which surely characterise governance at the present time – trust is at a premium. As we have seen, trust 'lubricates co-operation', reducing the need for checking, stalling, hedging – the vast array of actions we normally refer to as 'game playing'!

The downside of trusting is that it makes us vulnerable – it 'involves an estimation about whether the trustee will do something beneficial or detrimental before the truster can really know for sure' (Meyerson *et al.*, 1996: 176). We are open to exploitation, to being taken advantage of. In deciding whether to trust, both parties face a trade-off between autonomy, certainty and control on the one hand, and potential gains of efficiency and innovation on the other. In central/local relations it is not too strong to say that the two parties are used to expecting the worst of each other, in terms of both motivations and tactics. And for cat and mouse to learn to trust each other is a huge challenge. To keep on trusting each other may be even harder (as circumstances and priorities change), and yet a long-term perspective is vital to building trust. As Hirschman (1984) points out, trust is a unique and peculiar resource: it is increased rather than depleted by use. Trust that is not put into action dwindles to nothing. Trust is peculiarly hard to create when it does not already exist. At the same time, there exist many 'islands of trust' upon which new relationships can be built. As Lipnack and Stamps (1994:

196) argue in a business context, organisational cultures are 'storage vaults of social capital based on their history and current dynamics'. Are central and local government prepared to draw upon such resources to 'capitalise' new relationships?

Two Approaches to Understanding Trust: Bargaining and Belief, Policy and Passion

There are as many typologies of approaches to trust as there are academic articles on the subject. However, such classifications tend to cohere around a distinction between trust based upon *bargaining* and trust based upon *belief*. Powell (1996: 62), while using different terms, explains the key distinction thus:

- Bargaining – where trust is 'a rational outcome of an iterated chain of contacts in which farsighted parties recognise the potential benefits of their continued interaction';

- Belief – where trust is 'a by-product of the embeddedness of individuals in a web of social relations such that values and expectations are commonly shared'.

Dunn makes a similar point in explaining that trust can be both a 'policy' and a 'passion' (1993: 641).

The argument of this article is that both central and local government are serious in their desire to create and maintain greater trust in their relationships. However, tensions are arising because central and local government are working with two different conceptions of the origins and dynamics of trust. Central government sees trust as emerging out of a bargaining process: each 'side' has resources and competences that the other does not and, by recognising this interdependence and potential reciprocity, a more trusting and productive relationship can be achieved. Local government sees trust as emerging out of a consensus on common values: rebuilding trust between central and local government requires agreement on fundamental principles of local self-government, backed up by measures to restore discretion and capacity to local government. The discussion that follows illustrates the significance of the 'bargaining' and 'belief' stances within central/local relations, whilst also looking at the weaknesses of both positions and at emerging possibilities for a negotiated, middle-way to rebuilding trust.

REBUILDING TRUST?

In the classic study of central/local relations under the Conservatives, Loughlin, writing in 1996, claims that:

> In the new system ... there is little room for any sense of trust. Acting presumably on the basis that the idea of trust provides too insecure a foundation for the system, the Government has forged a hierarchical central/local relationship based on precise powers and duties. Discretion has been replaced by rules. (1996: 261)

This section considers progress towards restoring trust as a basis for central/local relations, in the context of New Labour's ambitious plans for democratic renewal.

A Change of Mood

While Labour's 1997 manifesto promised that local decision making would be 'less constrained by central government', the biggest change evident in the first months following the election was in the style and mood of central/local relations. As the newly ennobled Labour council leader, Steve Bassam, put it: 'The 18 year long war of attrition has gone, replaced by a more collaborative partnership-based approach between central and local government.' For its part, central government was quick to signal a new commitment to dialogue and consultation with local government. As Hilary Armstrong, Minister for Local Government, promised in a speech in June 1997: 'We are not just a new Government, we are a new type of Government ... Our decisions will not be handed down from on high ... We do not have a monopoly of wisdom and ideas. We want to hear your ideas and we want you to tell us what you think of ours.' Such sentiments appeared to signal a clear renewal of trust – that central government was willing to compromise on certainty and control in order to maximise exchange and learning. In the same speech, the new minister signalled her intention to create a new type of forum for central/local debate at the highest level:

> Let us sweep away the formal, ritualistic gatherings of ministers and local government leaders which I think we all agree have become rather pointless affairs. We would like to replace these sessions with more coherent and constructive contacts on main service issues and finance.

The 'central–local partnership' was created soon after the election, with a 'concordat' setting out the principles of consultation published in November 1997. The new arrangements were intended to focus top-level meetings on what Stewart (1996) has called the 'wicked issues', leaving nitty-gritty finance and service issues to forums involving civil servant and local government officers. Reflecting our earlier arguments, the need for negotiation over matters of detail was seen to recede in the context of greater trust, allowing for an emphasis on long-term planning and innovative approaches. As a DETR press release to mark the third meeting of the partnership explained:

> The meeting has the remit to consider the major issues involving local government, particularly those which cross departmental boundaries and require a Government-wide approach. The meeting is a forum for central and local government to work in partnership to tackle the multiple causes of social and economic decline and to improve local services. (3 March 1998)

Because trust is increased rather than depleted by use, the sheer volume of central/local contracts has constituted an important new development. Speaking about the ongoing review of local government finance at the Labour Local Government Conference in February 1998, the minister explained: 'I don't want to design a system from the top down, I want to design a system from the bottom up, drawing on your experiences.' Hilary Armstrong's personal commitment to consultation, her hectic schedule of speeches for local government events and her 'road-shows' around the country all indicated a 'new mood' in central/local relations. In more concrete terms, the first year of the new government saw consultation with local government on more than 20 individual policy initiatives, a referendum which found in favour of a new elected assembly (and mayor) for London, and the signing of the European Charter of Local Self-Government. The new policy style involved not only consultation with local government but support for the practical piloting of new approaches – for instance on Best Value, service improvement and, initially at least, new political management structures. Additional funding was made available at an early stage (notably as a result of the Comprehensive Spending Review), particularly for education, but also for housing, transport, regeneration, museums and the arts.

The publication in early 1998 of six consultation papers on local government 'modernisation' signalled that the reform process was not to be a piecemeal affair; nor would it dodge (as so many Conservative reviews had) the big questions concerning local government's fundamental role and purpose. The Green Papers covered local democracy and community leadership; improving local services through 'Best Value'; business rates; improving local financial accountability; capital finance; and a new ethical framework. Labour's second year in office saw the publication of a major White Paper, *Modern Local Government: In Touch with the People*, which has been followed by draft local government bills on Best Value and political leadership and 'standards'.

Local Government as a Partner in Change

The new mood in central/local relations has not, however, precluded demands for change within local government. As John Prescott put it when launching the Green Paper on democratic renewal (February 1998): 'This government believes in local government', but 'Be in no doubt we want to see change'. As we shall see later, the government's (increasingly) trenchant tone in demanding change has been seen by many in local government as at odds with the acclaimed spirit of 'partnership' in central/local relations. There are differences, however, between the Conservatives 'reform or die' message to local government and New Labour's approach to change.

First, *change is seen as the guarantor of a future for local government* – it is for local authorities' 'own good'. As Hilary Armstrong has put it: 'My aim is that authorities will be so respected by their local people that no central government will be able to come in again and undermine them like the last one did' (*Local Government Chronicle*, 6 Feb. 1998).

Second, *change must be 'owned' by local authorities themselves* – the government will lay down the parameters, but councils themselves must develop new ways of working (for instance, through piloting). At the Labour Local Government Conference in February 1998, Hilary Armstrong put it like this: 'Councils must cease to be the prisoners of their past and become the masters of their destiny, driving change not just responding to it.'

Third, *change will be spearheaded by democratic reforms*, in contrast to the primacy of managerialism within the Conservatives' approach. As Hilary Armstrong explained at Democracy Network's conference in January 1998: 'Democratic renewal is inextricably linked to other important initiatives: the introduction of best value; redressing the balance between local and centrally generated revenue; and removing crude and universal capping. So be in no doubt. We expect the debate on democratic reform to lead to real and meaningful changes.'

While central government wants to see change within local government, it also recognises that local government is an important *tool* for change. Central government needs local authorities – to deliver good local services, to flesh out and implement its grand schemes for education, health and 'welfare to work', and to show the public on a day-to-day basis that Labour and 'good government' go together. The government sees local authorities as key agents in the implementation of its election pledges. Where their Conservative predecessors sought to implement new policies through the creation of new local quangos which explicitly bypassed elected local authorities, Labour ministers recognise the potential value of working with local government to achieve their aims. At the Labour Local Government

Conference in February 1998, the Secretary of State for the Environment, Transport and the Regions underlined the important role that local government could play in the 'modernisation' of Britain. Speaking of new policies on crime, jobs, health, education and transport, John Prescott argued that 'We can only deliver these pledges effectively with the co-operation and involvement of local government'. Such statements appeared to indicate a renewal of trust in the sense of fostering expectations of interdependence and mutually beneficial action.

At the same time, New Labour has shown no enthusiasm for killing off the local quangos so often criticised whilst in opposition. Local authorities are seen as just one (albeit important) channel for service delivery and policy development. The Labour manifesto set out Labour's 'agnosticism' over preferred service providers in stating that: 'we see no reason why a service should be delivered directly (by local councils) if other more efficient means are available'. Tony Blair's pamphlet for the Institute of Public Policy Research (1998: 20) goes so far as to argue the case for transferring further functions to voluntary bodies and businesses, where individual local authorities are failing in terms of standards:

> The government will not hesitate to intervene directly to secure improvements where services fall below acceptable standards. And, if necessary, it will look to other authorities and agencies to take on duties where an authority is manifestly incapable of providing an effective service and unwilling to take the action necessary to improve its performance.

Recent developments on the implementation of the 'new deal' and on health and education improvement zones have demonstrated Labour's commitment to working through the mixed economy of local provision nurtured by the Tories. At the same time, the concept of Best Value – whilst replacing any requirement for external competition or contracting – explicitly recognises that local authority services may best be delivered in 'partnership' with other providers. However, in contrast to the Conservative perspective, New Labour's vision for local governance does not relegate elected local authorities to some kind of residual pick-up-the-pieces category. Rather, the fundamental purpose of elected local government is reasserted through a commitment to 'democratic renewal'. The future of local authorities, it is argued, lies in a reinvigorated role as community leaders and organs of public participation and representation.

Democratic Renewal

Echoing the long-term calls of commentators like Professors John Stewart and Gerry Stoker (see, for instance, Stewart and Stoker, 1995) and the work of the Commission for Local Democracy (see Pratchett and Wilson, 1996), the principle behind democratic renewal is that the unique role of elected local authorities lies not in their service delivery capacity but in their *potential* ability to represent and speak for their local communities. Whatever package of services local authorities deliver (or are ultimately responsible for), they are uniquely placed among other local agencies in terms of their democratic mandate. This mandate provides a basis from which the council can act as a broker of local partnerships and an advocate for its locality and the communities within it.

The government's stress upon local democracy as the *raison d'être* of local government is in stark contrast to the attempted 'managerialisation' of local politics under the Conservatives, which championed consumer choice and producer competition over party politics, local elections and public deliberation. New Labour's vision implies a greater degree of trust – local government is not simply a service delivery agent but a *bona fide* organ of government. As Tony Blair (1998: 13) explains: 'At the heart of local government's new role is leadership ... It will mean councils using their unique status and authority as directly elected bodies to develop a vision for their locality ... provide a focus for partnership (and) guarantee quality services for all.'

Proposals for democratic renewal fall into two main areas:

Public participation and consultation. The Green Paper on local democracy argues in favour of 'modernising electoral arrangements to improve the accountability of councils and to increase participation in local elections' (DETR, 1998a: para. 2.3). The subsequent White Paper confirms the government's preference for annual elections (to increase accountability) and its intention to legislate to allow experimentation in the conduct of elections (for example, on voting places, hours and days, postal and electronic voting), with the aim of increasing turnout (1998b). The Green Paper also argues that ongoing public involvement in the work of local authorities is 'crucial to the health of local democracy'. It proposes 'new ways in which councils can listen to their communities and involve local people in their decisions, and in their policy planning and review' (1998a: para. 2.3). The Green Paper recognises that many local authorities are experimenting with new forms of participation (for example, citizens' juries, focus groups and opinion polls) and discusses the value of developing a strategic approach to consultation which minimises social exclusion and maximises the potential for broader processes of citizen education (see Lowndes *et al.*, 1998). The White Paper signals the government's intention to impose a new statutory duty to consult and engage with local communities, crucially within the process of establishing

Best Value. Engagement with local citizens is also to be a criterion for the status of 'beacon council', whereby the best performing councils can win additional financial and operating discretion.

Political management and community leadership. The Green Paper argues in favour of 'devising new ways of working for councils, giving them clearer political and management structures' (1998a: para. 2.3). The White Paper moves from the language of experimentation and pilots to the more prescriptive requirement that councils introduce a split between executive and scrutiny/representative functions via one of three models (a directly elected mayor with cabinet, a cabinet with leader, or a directly elected mayor with council manager). The measure is intended to clarify accountability, revive public interest in local government, and produce a more independent and dynamic leadership able to represent communities locally and further afield. It is hoped that councillor recruitment and retention will benefit from the clarification of roles and the modernisation of arrangements for policy making and review. The draft Local Government Bill effectively compels councils to scrap existing structures (as explained in the commentary to the Bill, *Local Leadership, Local Choice*, DETR, 1999). It requires local authorities to consult with communities about how they are to be governed, offering a range of options for new political structures. The White Paper also confirms that there will be legislation placing councils under a new duty to promote the economic, social and environmental well being of their areas. It will be underpinned by new discretionary powers enabling councils to take steps in pursuit of the duty (whilst central government maintain reserve powers) and to engage in partnerships.

TRUST: BARGAINING OR BELIEF?

Despite the volume of activity and cascade of fine words, tensions have emerged in central/local relations. Central government is frustrated with the uneven pace of change among local authorities and with what it sees as a cautious, even defensive, response by local government to policy consultations. It is not prepared, as an article of belief, to restore powers or increased discretion to local government. It wants local government as a partner in its 'modernisation' programme, but not on any terms. For its part, local government is increasingly frustrated with the reluctance of central government to exercise *trust in practice*, which, as we saw earlier, involves a trade-off between certainty and control on the one hand, and innovation and risk-taking on the other. To capture the benefits from trust, agents 'on both sides' have to be prepared to face uncertainty and to make themselves vulnerable. While setting a context for renewed trust, central government seems to want to keep trust itself on hold – it is a prize for those authorities willing to embrace its new agenda. The article now explores the emerging tensions in central/local relations, showing how different approaches to trust are coming into conflict, with potentially damaging consequences for the democratic renewal agenda.

Sensitivities of Style

Despite the talk of a new mood in central/local relations, it is startling how many photographs in the local government press show ministers wagging a finger in the direction of a local authority audience. There is a hectoring, school teacherish tone to many of their exhortations. Launching the Green Paper on democratic renewal (February 1998), John Prescott told local government that it should 'Be in no doubt we want to see change'. In an interview the same month in *Local Government Chronicle*, Hilary Armstrong announced: 'What we are saying is do not believe reform isn't necessary. Reform is necessary. Reform is critical ... We want local government to be secure in the hearts and minds of local people, and nobody, but nobody, could say that is the case now' (6 Feb. 1998).

While the great majority of those in local government have no argument with the core content of the government's agenda for local government reform, many resent what they see as the unnecessarily negative picture that the government paints of local councils. Responding to the first of the consultative papers, the Labour Leader of Blackpool Borough Council argued that: 'Local government is not in the awful state that has been described. There should not be change for change's sake'. True, Tony Blair's 1998 pamphlet states that 'Local government at its best is brilliant and cannot be bettered'. However, the ever-present 'but...' serves to alienate, rather than motivate, many in local government. The government-sponsored 'spin' on the message of the pamphlet was all too clear in the media coverage – that local government is smug and needs a good kicking! Any reading of the key 'texts' on modernising local government will record the consistent ordering of two concepts: 'tackling performance failure and rewarding success', as Chapter 5 of the Best Value Green Paper puts it (see Game, 1998: 20).

The picture of backward, complacent local government which permeates many ministerial pronouncements seems odd given the extensive change that has occurred in local authorities over recent years. Much of this change was forced upon unwilling councils, but much has also been internally generated. There exists a vast reservoir of local government-owned good practice (LGMB, 1993; LGA/LGMB, 1998), much of which the government is drawing upon in its design and piloting of new approaches.

Innovative approaches to inter-agency working, to public consultation and
'empowerment', and to the design of new political and management
structures are hallmarks of the best local authorities – many of them Labour-
controlled. Local government's frustration at the dominance of negative
stereotypes is further fuelled by its knowledge of the far slower pace of
change in Whitehall and Westminster, and the seemingly less urgent
demands for reform in those quarters.

To central government, local authorities can appear excessively
defensive. The coverage of Blair's pamphlet in *Local Government
Chronicle*, for example, was unremittingly negative, focusing on the closing
comments about removing a local authority's powers in the context of
repeated failure. Local government's preoccupation with matters of belief –
for instance, the sacred cow of greater financial autonomy (discussed
below) – comes across to ministers as both unrealistic and arrogant,
reflecting councils' overblown sense of their own importance. Central
government has stated many times its commitment to the principles of local
democracy and self-government – in the Green and White Papers and
through the signing of the European Charter (refused under the
Conservatives) – and yet local government remains sceptical.

Local authorities' studied parochialism also annoys many in
Westminster and Whitehall. Research on public participation initiatives and
on new political management structures demonstrates a knee-jerk hostility
to new ideas emanating from the centre (see Lowndes *et al.*, 1998; Pratchett
et al., 1999). To take an example, the government has switched, in moving
from Green to White Papers and on to draft legislation, from encouraging
innovation in political management to requiring change. The justification?
The government would point to a singular lack of enthusiasm among the
vast majority of local authorities. Research in 1999 demonstrated that only
one per cent of councils was considering the introduction of a directly
elected mayor (Pratchett *et al.*, 1999), despite the government's promotion
of the idea and opinion poll evidence showing significant public support. In
the context of local government reactions to draft legislation, there are even
hints that the government may impose directly elected mayors in some
cities.

Financial Discretion

Nowhere are the contrasting approaches to trust more clearly demonstrated
than in the central/local debate over finance. Alongside compulsory
competitive tendering (CCT), it was the financial regime based upon
council tax capping, standard spending assessments, a nationalised business
rate and tightly controlled capital finance that came to epitomise the
Conservatives' attempt to emasculate local democracy. For local

government leaders, financial reform is not primarily a technical matter. The abolition of capping and the return of business rates to local authority control are seen as *necessary starting points* for democratic renewal – as key proofs of central government's trust. Responses to the first of the 1998 Green Papers demonstrate the argument:

> It is no good giving authorities a new look in terms of internal structures if they don't have the capacity to act decisively locally. That means greater financial autonomy. (Sir Jeremy Beecham, Chair of the Local Government Association)

> If you really want standards, if you really want democracy, you have got to trust us with money. Without that, talk of democracy and structures is nothing but a sham. (Labour Leader of Bury Metropolitan Council)

> They might talk to us and might smile at us but they may not actually do anything. Does government really trust us to make our own decisions and mistakes, tempered by democratic accountability? (David Williams, Liberal Democrat Group Leader, Local Government Association)

> Forget all the wonderful stuff ... about the splendours of service in local government and the need to give it a new lease of life. The plain fact is that Labour does not trust local government any more than the Conservatives did. (David Curry, former Conservative Local Government Minister)

The government's promise in the 1998 White Paper to abolish 'crude and universal capping' (whilst maintaining reserve powers) has gone some way to placate pragmatists in local government, especially in the context of the 'capping holiday' announced in the April 1999 financial settlement. At the same time, a lively debate on the localisation of the business rate in the pages of the *Local Government Chronicle* has served to illustrate different views regarding the link (or not) between local accountability and financial autonomy. In one corner, Professor Gerry Stoker has argued that, when local authorities are regarded primarily as community leaders rather than service providers, accountability becomes a 'subtle and complex concept' not reducible to (or requiring of) any straightforward link between representation and taxation. Accountability, Stoker argues, can be enhanced by a range of democratic reforms at the local level. In response to his critics in local government, Stoker suggests that 'Local government finance is in danger of becoming more a matter of theology than practical evidence-based policy making' (27 Nov. 1998).

In the other corner, Professor Robin Hambleton refutes the 'Stoker heresy' with a reassertion of the fundamental principles of the Layfield Report (1976). He argues that the decline in the last 30 years of the proportion of local spending funded out of rates, accompanied by capping, has led to an unacceptably low level of local authority discretion. Using poll data he points to a relationship between this decline and declining levels of public belief that local elections affect 'how things are run locally' (11 Dec. 1999). Unsurprisingly, it is the former argument that has found favour with a central government obsessed with issues of financial discipline – and voter attitudes to tax rises. For central government, there is no way in which a 'trusting' relationship with local government can be equated with significant increases in financial autonomy. For many local government leaders, the retention of reserve capping powers and the tightly restricted discretion over business rates (one per cent rise per annum over the national rate, rising to a maximum of five per cent over time) provide further evidence of the government's refusal to turn the rhetoric of trust into reality.

'Centralist Conditionality'

The idea of 'centralist conditionality' (Game, 1998: 26) aptly describes how many in local government (and some on the government's own backbenches) see the reality of central/local relations under New Labour. Considering first the charge of centralism, examples from finance and Best Value reforms serve as illustrations. The Green Paper *Modernising Local Government: Improving Local Financial Accountability* (1998c) actually argues that present legislation is 'too restrictive' regarding opportunities for ministerial intervention. The subsequent White Paper proposes broader powers (albeit to be used 'in reserve') 'to limit excessive council tax rises' (para. 5.12). On Best Value, the White Paper sets out a panoply of audit and inspection measures (paras. 7.35–7.45), alongside sweeping reserve powers of intervention (culminating in the transfer of functions to a third party in the case of serious service failures) (paras. 7.46–7.50). Many in local government are alarmed by the generally prescriptive nature of the Best Value regime (for example, the requirements for 'local performance plans' and a specific proportion of annual service reviews) and the 'intrusive and apparently continuous external presence' of auditors and inspectors (Game, 1998: 19). There also appears to be an underlying confusion as to who it is who actually decides whether Best Value is being achieved – local people (through consultation and electoral mechanisms) or government auditors and inspectors? (Game, 1998: 18). Both the finance and Best Value proposals make clear that reform is required to 'safeguard the Government's interests' (on tax-and-spend decisions and service standards – and associated voter perceptions!), as well as to restore and enhance local accountability. Determining the appropriate balance between these two objectives is a core tension within central/local relations.

The government's centralism has, however, a new sophistication. Central/local relations is becoming characterised by a policy style of 'selective concessions' and 'selective retribution' (Game, 1998: 26). The 'best performing' local authorities will be rewarded with new powers – primarily through the Beacon Council scheme but also through pilot projects and competitive funding regimes. At the same time, 'failing' and 'over-spending' councils will be subject to direct intervention, and ultimately the removal of functions. Powers of intervention are to be held 'in reserve' and used selectively rather than applied across the board. A local government cynic may see the approach as one of 'divide and rule', aimed at avoiding the sort of implementation failures that accompanied the Conservatives' 'blunt hammer' approach (witnessed most famously over the poll tax). However, it is clear that the favoured policy style represents not just a new approach to implementation but also to understanding the role of local government within a 'modern' British democracy. The government's conception of trust within central/local relations becomes clearer in the context of an emerging bargain – democracy for discretion.

Democracy for Discretion

New Labour's concern with renewing local democracy is clearly infused as much with *realpolitik* as with any idealistic commitment to local self-government. While the public may have more interest in national than local elections, day-to-day contacts between citizens and the state are overwhelmingly concentrated at the local level (Lowndes, 1995; Parry *et al.*, 1992). The public is not always aware of which services are the responsibility of which tier of government. In short, people's experience of local government affects how they regard government in general. In addition, the public does not necessarily discriminate between the performance of a political party at the national and the local level. How New Labour is seen to be doing at the national level is affected by citizens' perceptions of the Labour-controlled councils on their doorsteps.

Making a reality out of Labour's promise of a new bond of trust with the British people requires a more open and a more trusted *local* government. It is difficult for central government to develop ways of consulting the public on a regular basis about the everyday issues which affect them (although not impossible – as in the use of opinion polls, focus groups and the new 'People's Panel'). It is in the style and outcome of local decision-making and service delivery that people are most likely to become aware of any greater openness in government or renewed bond of trust between government and citizen.

So, democratic renewal is not a local government policy *per se* – it is part of a much broader New Labour project. It is not the principle of local self-government that is being championed so much as the need for governance in general to become more porous, accountable and responsive: a reformed local government has an important role to play in this. Referring to the effects of centralisation under the Conservatives, Hilary Armstrong clearly sees the problem not as one of reduced local government autonomy but of reduced accountability and public involvement: 'we believe that the balance has slipped too far to the centre and that central government has taken too many powers to itself and left local people out of the loop' (interview in *Local Government Chronicle*, 6 Feb. 1998).

A 1996 piece by the think-tank Demos argues against seeing greater local autonomy or discretion in terms of 'theological ideas', 'blueprints' or 'settlements':

> myths of 'self-government' are as dangerous at the local level as they are at the level of the nation state. In a time of growing transnational interdependence and external constraint, claims of autonomy and governing power are not absolutes, but make sense only in complex and ever-shifting structures of interlocking power, competence and legitimacy. (Mulgan and 6, 1996: 3)

Greater autonomy for local government is seen as conditional upon criteria of 'competence and legitimacy'. Democratic renewal, coupled with ever improving service standards, is seen as the price that local government must pay for increased freedom of action. Also, because 'local government' is not a principle in itself, local authorities must be prepared to be assessed *individually* in terms of their particular achievements regarding 'competence and legitimacy'. The Demos article again captures perfectly the sentiment behind the government's reform agenda: 'Local authorities can once again become local *government*, but they must expect to earn that right, and earn it individually, and service by service. They must not be permitted to assume that it is theirs by inheritance' (Mulgan and 6, 1996: 7).

Ministerial pronouncements clearly reflect the idea that local government must 'earn' a restoration of key powers, and that 'good' authorities will be able to earn faster than 'bad' ones. While democratic renewal provides an opportunity for beleaguered local authorities to reassert their role and identity, it could also provide central government with the biggest stick yet with which to beat them (because it is the most fundamental)! At the start of the 1998 consultation process on 'modernisation', ministers put their point thus:

> Certain discretions or powers could be available to councils who could demonstrate they were effectively involving their local

communities in their local decision-making. Such incentive arrangements would have the logic that the greater a council's democratic legitimacy, the greater scope it would follow to act for the benefit of its community. (John Prescott)

I see little point in giving extra powers to councils which are not dealing adequately with the powers they already have. But equally there's no reason why councils performing well should be held back by those who aren't. (Tony Blair)

We are all trusted according to what we deliver. (Hilary Armstrong)

Tensions between central and local government focus less on the detail of the reform measures proposed, and more on the nature of the bargain that is emerging. At the nub of the problem is a chicken and egg situation. Many in local govt believe they can do little to change relationships with their communities until they have more autonomy, crucially over revenue. This view is in direct contradiction to the government's position that local authorities must *prove* their suitability for increased powers through establishing a new relationship with their communities (while 'failing authorities' will be dealt with harshly). There is, for local authorities, a growing sense of unease about what could be called the 'testing and judging' process on democratic renewal. How will the quality of local democracy – in its broadest sense – be judged? And for how long are local authorities to be on trial? How is central government to 'prove' its side of the bargain – that it will use its powers fairly and wisely? The much-vaunted principles of trust and partnership seem to sit uneasily with central government's emerging discourse of incentives, threats and proofs.

CONCLUSION

The goal of a new trusting relationship between central and local government is, in theory, shared among all three main political parties and welcomed at central and local level alike. *Rebuilding Trust* was the title of the report published under the last Conservative government from the House of Lords Select Committee on Relations between Central and Local Government, under the cross-bencher Lord Hunt (House of Lords, 1996). William Hague recently committed his party to become 'a friend of local institutions against the centralised state' (Conservative Local Government Conference, Feb. 1998). So what is the likelihood of this aspiration becoming reality?

As we have seen, there are many positive indications: the signing of the European Charter on Local Self-Government; the new top-level 'partnership' arrangements; extensive consultation and plans for legislation on a wide range of local government matters; and the ground-level developments in planning for Best Value, democratic renewal and new approaches to health, education, employment and community safety. The government's concerns with central/local dialogue, the use of pilots, and the potential role of local authorities as 'community leaders' all serve to illustrate its preparedness to trust local councils, and to value their local expertise and democratic mandate. So why the mounting frustration on each side? We have seen how central and local government are approaching the issue of trust in different ways, leading to conflicting expectations and priorities. For central government, greater local autonomy and new powers will follow only after local authorities have proved their commitment to change, particularly in terms of renewing relationships with local communities. Trust will emerge out of this bargaining process – democracy for discretion – as each 'side' recognises the benefits of continued interaction. For its part, local government wants the government to grant it greater autonomy and new powers as an expression of a shared commitment to the principle of local self-government, so ravaged under successive Conservative governments. Rather than seeing trust as the outcome of a bargain, local authorities have expected to see a trust based upon shared understandings and values. Crucially, they see trust as the starting point rather than the goal of a new central/local relationship.

What is clear is that local and central government are in the process of negotiating a new relationship of trust – the current frustrations are part of that process. There would be advantages, however, in both 'sides' re-evaluating their approach to trust. To capture the potential benefits from trust – including reduced transactions costs and an increased capacity for innovation and risk-taking – both 'bargaining' and 'belief' approaches need to be challenged. According to Powell (1996: 63), to see trust as emerging out of a bargain is to overstate 'the ability of parties to take the long-term view and practice mutual forbearance'. Current relations between central and local government illustrate this limitation only too well! At the same time, to see trust as emerging from belief alone is to understate 'the extent to which co-operation is buttressed by sustained contact, regular dialogue, and constant monitoring'. Trust cannot be built solely on the basis of a bargain or a principle – in fact, it grows out of ongoing interaction and learning. As Powell (1996: 63) explains:

> In short ... it is misleading to regard trust as either an outcome derived from calculation or a value traced to culture ... [W]e need to recognise the extent to which trust is neither chosen nor embedded but is instead learned and reinforced, hence the product of ongoing interaction and discussion.

To end on an overtly prescriptive note, local government needs to remind itself that trust has to be actively made and remade – it cannot be guaranteed on the basis of an abstract, historical principle. Trust needs living institutions to support it. At the same time, central government needs to remind itself that trust emerges organically out of ongoing interaction and discussion between parties: it cannot be rationed out 'as and when' by a dominant partner. 'Both 'sides' must remember that to trust is to make oneself vulnerable, to face uncertainty and to take risks. Despite the irritation creeping into much of the rhetoric of central/local relations (on both sides), there is in reality much to build on. Local and central government *are* engaged together in building new institutions for governance – in work on Best Value, cross-cutting issues, democratic renewal and constitutional change – and it is out of this day-to-day interaction that trust can be rebuilt. In the meantime, the process may be smoothed if central government learns to take greater account of local sensibilities, and local government learns to balance paranoia with patience. More concretely, local government will continue to look for some restoration of financial discretion, while central government will look for evidence that local authorities are taking seriously the agenda for Best Value and democratic renewal.

The 'prize' for rebuilding trust is potentially far greater than the smoothing of relations between central and local government. Trust is the potential core of a new 'governing code' for the twenty-first century – a code able to reconnect the multifarious agencies of government with the disparate communities that constitute the 'public'. Democratic renewal, in its broadest sense, is contingent upon rebuilding trust in governance.

NOTES

Thanks are due to the Local Government Management Board (now the Improvement and Development Agency) which provided funding for the initial work on which this article is based. An earlier version of the argument is published as: 'Rebuilding Trust?' in *Two to Tango? Charting the Central-Local Relationship and its Legal Framework* (London: Local Government Management Board, 1998).

REFERENCES

Best, M., 1990, *The New Competition* (Cambridge: Polity Press).

Blair, T., 1998, *Leading the Way: A New Vision for Local Government* (London: Institute for Public Policy Research).

Creed, W. and R. Miles, 1996, 'Trust in Organizations', in R. Kramer and T. Tyler (eds.), *Trust in Organizations* (London: Sage).

Department of the Environment, Transport and the Regions, 1998a, *Modernising Local Government: Local Democracy and Community Leadership* (London: DETR).

Department of the Environment, Transport and the Regions, 1998b, *Modern Local Government: In Touch with the People* (London: DETR).

Department of the Environment, Transport and the Regions, 1998c, *Modernising Local Government: Improving Local Financial Accountability* (London: DETR).

Department of the Environment, Transport and the Regions, 1999, *Local Leadership, Local Choice* (London: DETR).

Dunn, J., 1993, 'Trust', in R. Goodin and P. Pettit (eds.), *A Companion to Contemporary Political Philosophy* (Oxford: Basil Blackwell).

Etzioni, A., 1995, *The Spirit of Community* (London: Fontana).

Gambetta, D., 1988, 'Can we Trust Trust?', in D. Gambetta (ed.), *Trust: Making and Breaking Co-operative Relations* (Oxford: Basil Blackwell).

Game, C., 1998, 'Carrots and Semtex: New Labour's Modernisation Agenda for British Local Government', Paper presented to the Annual Conference of the International Association of Schools and Institutes of Administration, Paris, September.

Granovetter, M., 1985, 'Economic Action and Social Structure: The Problem of Embeddedness', *American Journal of Sociology*, Vol.78, No.6, pp.481–510.

Hirschman, A., 1984, 'Against Parsimony: Three Easy Ways of Complicating Some Categories of Economic Discourse, *American Economic Review*, No.74, pp.88–96.

House of Lords, 1996, *Select Committee on Relations between Central and Local Government, Vols.I-III* (London: HMSO).

Lipnack, J. and J. Stamps, 1994, *The Age of the Network* (New York: Wiley).

Local Government Association/Local Government Management Board, 1998, *Democratic Practice: A Guide* (London: LGA/LGMB).

Local Government Management Board, 1993, *Fitness for Purpose* (London: LGMB).

Loughlin, M., 1996, *Legality and Locality: The Role of Law in Central/Local Government Relations* (Oxford: Clarendon Press).

Lowndes, V., 1995, 'Citizenship and Urban Politics'. in D. Judge, G. Stoker and H. Wolman (eds.), *Theories of Urban Politics* (London: Sage).

Lowndes, V. *et al.*, 1998, *Enhancing Public Participation in Local Government* (London: DETR).

Lowndes, V. and C. Skelcher, 1998, 'The Dynamics of Multi-Organisational Partnerships: An Analysis of Changing Modes of Governance', *Public Administration*, Vol.76, No.2, pp.313–34.

Meyerson, D., K. Weik and R. Kramer, 1996, 'Swift Trust and Temporary Groups', in R. Kramer and T. Tyler (eds.), *Trust in Organizations* (London: Sage).

Mulgan, G. and P. 6, 1996, 'The Local's Coming Home: Decentralisation by Degrees', *Demos*, 9, pp.3–7.

Parry, G., G. Moyser and N. Day, 1992, *Political Participation and Democracy in Britain* (Cambridge: Cambridge University Press).

Powell, W., 1996, 'Trust-Based Forms of Governance', in R. Kramer and T. Tyler (eds.), *Trust in Organizations* (London: Sage).

Powell, W., 1991, 'Neither Market nor Hierarchy: Network Forms of Organisation', in G. Thompson *et al.* (eds.), *Markets, Hierarchies and Networks: The Co-ordination of Social Life* (Buckingham: Open University Press).

Pratchett, L. *et al.*, 1999, *Political Management Arrangements: The Position at the Start of 1999* (London: Local Government Association/Improvement and Development Agency).

Pratchett, L. and D. Wilson (eds.), *Local Democracy and Local Government* (London: Macmillan).

Putnam, R., 1995, 'Tuning In, Turning Out: The Strange Disappearance of Social Capital in America', *PS: Political Science and Policy*, Vol.28, No.4.

Rhodes, R., 1999, 'Foreword: Governance and Networks', in G. Stoker (ed.), *The New Management of British Local Government* (London: Macmillan).

Rhodes, R., 1997, *Understanding Governance* (Buckingham: Open University Press).

Stewart, J., 1996, *Local Government Today* (London: LGMB).

Stewart, J. and G. Stoker, 1995, *Local Government in the 1990s* (London: Macmillan).

Stoker, G., 1999, 'Capitalise on Community', *Local Government Chronicle*, 6 Jan.

Tam, H., 1997, *Communitarianism* (London: Macmillan).

Abstracts

Introduction: Defining Democratic Renewal, *by Lawrence Pratchett*

Democratic renewal is one of New Labour's central policy initiatives yet its meaning remains ambiguous. This article introduces the other contributions in this volume by exploring three definitions of the subject. First, it defines democratic renewal as a set of practical solutions for the perceived problems of contemporary local democracy: electoral reform, enhanced public participation, improved political management structures and new community leadership. Second, it defines it in terms of broader political, cultural and constitutional change: as an attempt to modify attitudes towards Britain's democratic institutions by engendering higher levels of social capital. Finally, it defines it as a process of creating a new mode of local democracy in which various components of direct, consultative, deliberative and representative democracy are mixed to create a radically different democratic polity.

The Key Themes of Democratic Renewal, *by Hilary Armstrong MP*

The contents of the Local Government White Paper *Modern Local Government: In Touch with the People* have been widely discussed so the article does not spell out its contents in detail or run through its main proposals. Instead, it sketches out the political themes which the author believes *In Touch with the People* represents and the opportunities for local government which they present. Those themes are: redefining the relationship of local government with the people; earning public expenditure; ending ideological battles over public service provision; and innovation in governance.

Democratic Renewal in Local Government: Continuity and Change, *by Andrew Gray and Bill Jenkins*

Assessing the British government's programme for democratic renewal in local government requires a recognition that local self-government is distinguished from other forms of local governance by the elected basis of relatively autonomous multi-purpose authorities. Its contribution to the democratic state may be functional in promoting self-government or dysfunctional in promoting differentiation and inequality of area. Thus New Labour faces an old dilemma. Resolving it may require a consideration of participation and especially alienation and an assessment of the extent to which more or less devolution to local authorities serves the priorities of our time.

Public Participation and the Democratic Renewal Agenda: Prioritisation or Marginalisation? *by Steve Leach and Melvin Wingfield*

The White Paper *Modern Local Government: In Touch with the People* contains a range of proposals for modernising British local government. Some are concerned with improving the quality, cost-effectiveness and responsiveness of local services. Other proposals, however, are concerned with the constitutional position of local government, which for various reasons is viewed as in need of 'democratic renewal'. There are four key elements to the democratic renewal programme aimed at developing opportunities for citizens to participate in local government. This article summarises the main trends emerging from a recent DETR-commissioned research project on the forms of participation being carried out by local authorities, and exposes some of the tensions and contradictions of public participation in the context of the wider democratic renewal agenda.

Researching Public Participation, *by Marian Barnes*

Interest in the practical development of new ways of involving citizens has been accompanied by a wish on the part of those investing in such processes to know if they worked and if they made a difference. This is usually constructed as a need to undertake evaluations of different methods of enabling public participation. However, questions about effectiveness of different methods need to reflect the nature and purpose of different approaches. The exploration of these types of issue may be better understood as a process of researching rather than evaluating. In this context the article offers six criteria for evaluating fora in which deliberation takes place.

The Party Group: A Barrier to Democratic Renewal, *by Colin Copus*

The political party group is the most important place in which councillors consider and debate local issues, decide political tactics and, in the majority group, make political decisions. Group processes are private. Moreover, party groups demand, and receive, members' loyalty over and above even the wishes of the councillor's own electorate. This paper considers councillors' group loyalty and its impact on the democratic renewal project. It examines how groups could react to maintain influence under new political management, and argues that whilst the democratic renewal debate has so far largely ignored the party group, it represents a barrier to that project. Moreover, new models of political management generate pressures that, far from opening up local political processes, will drive them further into the privacy of the group.

Political Leadership in the New Urban Governance: Britain and France Compared, *by Peter John and Alistair Cole*

The tension between leadership and democracy is always implicit in the governance of the contemporary city. The qualities that make local political systems work are the same ones that can undermine the claims of liberal democracy to be an effective and responsive type of government. Yet there are circumstances when strong leadership combines with effective democratic control. In particular, we argue in this paper that there are creative pathways that local political leaders may take to mobilise local communities for collective action; and skilful leaders can raise the governing capacity of local communities. To achieve these contradictory aims, there are a variety of leadership styles that emerge in different contexts, and each has its costs and benefits.

Rebuilding Trust in Central/Local Relations: Policy or Passion? *by Vivien Lowndes*

This article argues that both central and local government are serious in their desire to rebuild trust. Tensions have arisen, however, because each 'side' is working with a different conception of trust. Central government sees trust as emerging out of a bargaining process – greater local autonomy will follow only when local authorities prove their commitment to change. Local government sees renewed trust (and enhanced local discretion) as a matter of belief, reflecting principles of local self-government. Exploring developments in central/local relations since 1997, the article identifies the weaknesses of both positions and considers the possibility of a negotiated, middle way to rebuilding trust. The article argues that democratic renewal, in its broadest sense, is contingent upon rebuilding trust in governance.

Notes on Contributors

Hilary Armstrong MP is Minister of State for Local Government and Regions.

Marian Barnes is Director of Social Research in the Department of Social Policy and Social Work, University of Birmingham. Much of her work over the last 12 years has been on user involvement and the self organisation of service users within a community care policy context. More recently her work has broadened to include public participation within the NHS and the development of new forms of democratic practice throughout the public sphere.

Colin Copus is head of the local government research unit at the University of Wolverhampton's Business School where he is a lecturer in public policy and politics. He has extensively researched party politics in local government and the organisation, activities and influence of the political party group. He has served as a London Borough councillor, a county councillor and district councillor and has chaired a major council committee.

Andrew Gray is Professor of Public Sector Management at the University of Durham. His research interests focus on the management of the mixed economies of public services, not least the challenges in being 'Business-like but not like a Business' (CIPFA, 1998).

Bill Jenkins is Reader in Public Policy and Management at the University of Kent. He has published widely (with Andrew Gray) on a range of topics relating to developments in public administration and public management in the UK, policy analysis and public policy evaluation.

Peter John is Reader in Politics and Sociology at Birkbeck College, University of London. He is author of *Analysing Public Policy* (London: Cassell, 1998) and articles in the *British Journal of Political Science*, *Urban Affairs Review*, *Urban Studies*, and other journals.

Steve Leach is Professor of Local Government at De Montfort University, Leicester, and was a member of the research team which carried out the DETR-sponsored research on public participation. He is currently working with several local authorities on different aspects of the democratic renewal agenda.

Vivien Lowndes is Professor of Local Government Studies at De Montfort University, Leicester. Her research interests include public participation and citizenship, partnerships, and management change in local government.

Lawrence Pratchett is a Senior Research Fellow in local government at De Montfort University, Leicester. His research interests include democratic renewal, public participation and ethics in modern governance. He is convenor of the Urban Politics Group of the Political Studies Association.

Melvin Wingfield is a Research Fellow in the Department of Public Policy, De Montfort University. He has wide-ranging research interests in local government but specialises in the politics of small rural authorities.

Index

Books of Related Interest

Managing Local Services
From CCT to Best Value
George A. Boyne, *Cardiff Business School* (Ed.)

The Labour Government has introduced legislation to place a new duty of Best Value on local authorities and to abolish Compulsory Competitive Tendering. In this book the implications of this policy change are analysed. The main differences between CCT and Best Value are identified, and the development of the new regime in England, Wales and Scotland is evaluated. The book also contains case studies of the implementation of Best Value in specific authorities.

144 pages   1999
0 7146 5020 X cloth
0 7146 8075 3 paper
A special issue of the journal Local Government Studies

QUANGOS and Local Government
A Changing World
Howard Davis, *University of Birmingham* (Ed.)

This publication seeks to develop understanding of the changing world of local governance and thus contribute to wider debates. The impact of these changes will continue to be felt for many years to come – whoever is in government.

104 pages   1996
0 7146 4735 7 cloth
0 7146 4324 6 paper
A special issue of the journal Local Government Studies

FRANK CASS PUBLISHERS
Newbury House, 900 Eastern Avenue, Ilford, Essex, IG2 7HH
Tel: +44 (0)20 8599 8866 Fax: +44 (0)20 8599 0984 E-mail: info@frankcass.com
NORTH AMERICA
5804 NE Hassalo Street, Portland, OR 97213 3644, USA
Tel: 800 944 6190 Fax: 503 280 8832 E-mail: cass@isbs.com
Website: www.frankcass.com

Local Government Reorganisation
The Review and its Aftermath

Edited by **Steve Leach**, *De Montfort University*

The Local Government Review has not been a rewarding experience for the majority of authorities who were drawn into it. Although those authorities which have achieved unitary status are generally positive about the outcome, elsewhere the Review has generated frustration, loss of morale and a sense of injustice.

The LGR provides an invaluable learning opportunity for academics and practitioners alike. It is only now that the Review is over that it is possible to interpret the process (with the benefit of hindsight) in a holistic way.

The Review is of particular interest to academics because it raises issues of political process and provides a test-bed for a range of decision-making theories. The interest to practitioners, in addition to the insights provided by academic analysis, lies in the highlighting of the lessons to be learned. This volume attempts to respond to both these perspectives.

The LGR may be over, but it leaves in its wake a whole range of unresolved dilemmas and unanswered questions. This volume aims to provide at least some clarification of and insight into a strange and complex process and to emphasise the lessons to be learned.

160 pages   1998
0 7146 4859 0 cloth

FRANK CASS PUBLISHERS
Newbury House, 900 Eastern Avenue, Ilford, Essex, IG2 7HH
Tel: +44 (0)20 8599 8866 Fax: +44 (0)20 8599 0984 E-mail: info@frankcass.com
NORTH AMERICA
5804 NE Hassalo Street, Portland, OR 97213 3644, USA
Tel: 800 944 6190 Fax: 503 280 8832 E-mail: cass@isbs.com
Website: www.frankcass.com